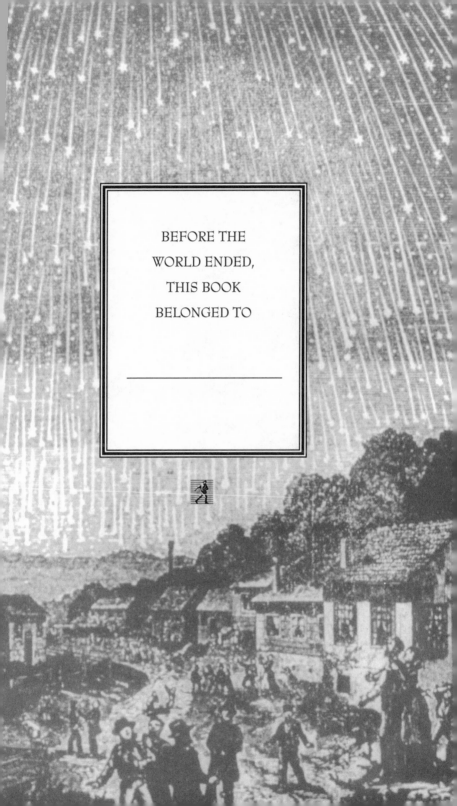

BEFORE THE
WORLD ENDED,
THIS BOOK
BELONGED TO

_____

Apocalypse
Wow!

APOCALYPSE WOW!

A Memoir for the End of Time

JAMES FINN GARNER

SIMON & SCHUSTER

SIMON & SCHUSTER
Rockefeller Center
1230 Avenue of the Americas
New York, New York 10020

This book is a work of fiction. Names, characters, places, and incidents either are products of the author's imagination or are used fictitiously. Any resemblance to actual events or locales or persons, living or dead, is entirely coincidental.

SIMON & SCHUSTER and colophon are registered trademarks of Simon & Schuster Inc.

Produced by Cader Books
Illustrations by Ron Barrett
Designed by Charles Kreloff

Manufactured in the United States of America

1 3 5 7 9 10 8 6 4 2

Library of Congress Cataloging-in-Publication Data is available.

ISBN 0-684-83649-1

The author gratefully acknowledges permission from Henry Holt & Co. to reprint "Fire and Ice" by Robert Frost from *The Poetry of Robert Frost,* edited by Edward Connery Lathem. Copyright 1916, 1923, 1928, 1930, 1934, 1939, 1947, ©1967, 1969 by Holt, Rinehart and Winston; copyright ©1964, 1967, 1970, 1975 by Leslie Frost Ballantine. Reprinted by permission of Henry Holt & Co. (p.VIII).

John Easter Youthbone's "End-Times Index" was inspired by Todd Strandberg's Web site, *The Rapture Index,* which can be found at http://www.novia.net/~todd/

CONTENTS

Some say the world will end in fire,
some say in ice.
From what I've tasted of desire
I hold with those that favor fire.
But if it had to perish twice,
I think I know enough of hate
To say that for destruction ice
Is also great
And would suffice.

—Robert Frost

[The end of the world] doesn't much concern me. I live
in Boston.

—Theodore Parker

SHOULD YOU BOTHER WITH THAT FIVE-YEAR CD?

THE OTHER DAY, I was unpacking a new waffle maker my wife and I had received as a gift. Among all the manuals, coupons, and other scraps of paper in the box, I found the warranty card. In large red letters, the card screamed at me:

**YOUR WAFFLE WIZARD IS GUARANTEED
UNTIL THE YEAR 2000!**

I thought to myself: "Wow. Barring manufacturing defects and any abuse on my part, I'll be able to enjoy hot, crunchy waffles into the next millennium."

My heart was both cheered and chilled by this.

I don't know about you, but this whole end-of-the-century thing really crept up on me. When I was a kid, it was fun to imagine where, who, and what I would be in the year 2000. Now I felt very unprepared for such a momentous event. Had I really gotten so caught up in my ballroom-dancing and pet-massage classes that I didn't notice it? And not only is it the end of the century, it's also the end of the millennium, when the grand odometer rolls over and every single one of us—king and

Time is not on our side.

commoner, president and special prosecutor—will have to order new checks from the bank so the date line can start with a 2. More than anything you might think of, this transition will be a once-in-a-lifetime event (unless you pull a Disney and dive into a cryogenic deep-freeze until the year 2100, or even 3000).

So I began to research just what this Year 2000 thing was all about. You hold the results of that research in your hands. The truth may shock you. So will *Apocalypse Wow!*

You may already be slightly familiar with this topic. It's been all over the news, directly and indirectly. Humanity is teetering on the brink of . . . well, *something*.

- ☄ The people of the Branch Davidian sect in Waco believed the end times were already here, as neatly outlined in the Bible. They were so distraught that they chose to follow an oversexed John Lennon wannabe with a Weird Al Yankovic haircut into their own Armageddon (conveniently supplied by the government).

- ☄ In Japan, members of the Aum Shinrikyo cult believed they could jump-start the apocalypse by releasing homemade nerve gas in the subways of Tokyo. They also believed their corpulent leader, Shoko Asahara, could float by meditating and that they could synchronize their brain waves with his by wearing battery-operated "electron hats."

- ☄ Both ultra-orthodox Jews and fundamentalist Christians are working to rebuild Solomon's temple on its original site in Jerusalem. (Before you applaud the altruism of the Christians, remember, this is no Habitat for Humanity project. They are doing this so that Christ can return and bring down our collective curtains.)

☙ Some experts (a term that you will find used very flexibly in this book) state that the earth will witness physical catastrophes from passing asteroids, top-heavy polar ice caps, rampant plagues, overpopulation, pollution, television retrospectives, and the reemergence of the lost continent of Atlantis. The partisans rooting for Godzilla have yet to be heard from, but there's still time.

But are we going to let all this bad news ruin things for us? If this world is going to blow up, let's go out with a bang! The Artist Formerly Known as Prince, as he sang in the hit "1999," knows this is going to be the party to end all parties: "I got a lion in my pocket, and baby, he's ready to roar!"❡

To usher in the 21st century with a grand New Year's Eve, many people are planning mega-blowouts for 1999.❡❡ The Millennium Society has been busy for a decade planning elaborate parties for that December 31. They will begin in New Zealand, then move to the Sydney Opera House, the Great Wall of China, the Taj Mahal, the Great Pyramid of Cheops, the Eiffel Tower, Stonehenge, Times Square, and Hawaii. A party in every time

❡For help in deciphering this and other obscure lines of prophecy, turn to "Prophecy: The Heavy Hitters" on page XXIX.

❡❡To all the pedants out there who are sharpening their pencils to write a letter of complaint: I *know* that the 21st century technically doesn't begin until January 1, 2001. I also know that "anal retentive" is hyphenated when used as an adjective. So lighten up.

Actually it isn't always: That man is anal retentive. He's an anal-retentive man. —Copy Ed.

XI

zone! Think of the frequent-flyer miles you could rack up! That is, of course, if the earth isn't destroyed first.

So slap on your rocket packs, kids, and blast off with me as we try and figure out just what will go down when the year 2000 pounces on us. Prepare to be shocked, enlightened, and stimulated. Clues to our collective fate have been included in the Bible, built into the dimensions of the Great Pyramid, and revealed to seers and psychics for decades. All it takes to discern these mysteries is an open mind and a credulous nature. If you've bought this book, you're halfway there.

A word of warning: This quest is not for the timid, the conventional, or the easily offended. The end of the world ain't no walk in the park. I don't need to point out that things *eschatological* (concerning the end times) and *scatological* (concerning bodily functions) are separated only by a single syllable.

And if at any time you are overwhelmed by the evidence presented here and begin to feel like all the certainties of your world are being knocked away like tenpins, put this book down and take a walk outside. Look up at the stars, consider the vastness of the universe, and say to yourself, "Well, so much for this!"

What Time Is It?

The year 2000 really is:

4698 in the Chinese calendar
(the Year of the Dragon)

5760/61 in the Hebrew calendar

1421 A.H. in the Islamic calendar

1993 for extreme procrastinators

A time for new stationery at 20th Century Fox

Doomsday Final Exam
Test Your End-Times IQ!!

1. What are the names of the Four Horsemen of the Apocalypse?
   a. War, Famine, Pestilence, and Death
   b. John, Paul, George, and Ringo
   c. Plague, Strife, Starvation, and Arsenio
   d. Manny, Moe, Jack, and Death

2. How many rabbis sit in Zurich and control the world's banking activities?
   a. Thirteen
   b. Four, with seven during peak hours and a half-day on Saturdays for your convenience
   c. Only 12; the 13th one has to stand because of this pain in his back, which is killing him, oy!
   d. Yeah, sure, like they'd let anyone know

3. What is meant by the term Rapture?
   a. The ascension of all true Christians before the beginning of the strife and tribulation caused by the Antichrist
   b. The feeling you get when you turn off The 700 Club
   c. A new fragrance from Calvin Klein
   d. A medical condition that requires a truss

4. If you are driving on the highway when the Rapture comes, and other drivers are pulled bodily out of their cars to heaven, what's the best course of action?
   a. Pull over to the side of the road until the driverless traffic stops
   b. Look for a nicer make of car than yours, drive alongside, and climb in
   c. Speed like hell, because the highway patrol will be too busy to stop you
   d. Repent your sins and head for the nearest Stuckey's

5. The great mystic Nostradamus predicted that the world
would end via
    a. a "King of Terror" appearing in the sky
    b. "Ghost Riders" appearing in the sky
    c. botulism
    d. a lack of interest

6. Many prominent astronomers now admit that the earth
will be devastated by a gigantic asteroid, and that this
will happen
    a. soon
    b. very soon
    c. extremely soon
    d. today
    e. yesterday

7. Which of the following should be considered absolutely
essential for your bomb shelter provisions?
    a. water purification pills
    b. canned vegetables
    c. first-aid kit
    d. Yahtzee

8. One of the basic tenets of the imminent earth changes
is the pole shift, which is
    a. a radical displacement of the earth's geographic
       poles from their present position
    b. the 8-to-4 workers in a Chicago sausage factory
    c. a demographic change in Hamtramck
    d. something baseball players often do in the batter's
       box

9. Quartz crystals are a good source of spiritual energy
because
    a. their perfectly geometric cellular structure allows
       them to receive and store psychic vibrations
    b. they make nicer jewelry than D-cell batteries
    c. they're safer than sticking a fork in your toaster
    d. they're just so shiny and stuff

10. Who is the Whore of Babylon mentioned in the Book of Revelation?
   a. the Pope
   b. the Antipope
   c. Sinéad O'Connor
   d. a certain favorite "advisor" to Saddam Hussein and his buddies

11. Christian fundamentalists believe the Bible is the literal, unerring word of God because
   a. it says so, right there in the Bible
   b. their parents said so
   c. they would be so heartbroken if no one ever found Noah's Ark
   d. it's easier than thinking

12. The number of the Beast of the Apocalypse is
   a. 666
   b. 999
   c. PEnnsylvania 6-5000
   d. unlisted

13. The first insight in James Redfield's The Celestine Prophecy is
   a. A spiritual awakening is occurring in human culture, brought about by a critical mass of individuals who experience their lives as a spiritual unfolding, a journey in which they are led forward by mysterious circumstances
   b. Same as above, plus an emphasis on the health benefits of cooking with hot peppers
   c. Hair spray can help remove ink stains on fabric before washing
   d. "Hey, this New Age publishing racket isn't so tough after all"

14. Are the people of the earth reaching a shared consciousness, wherein our converging psychic energy will eliminate strife and lead us into a new golden age?
    a. Yes
    b. Yes, absolutely
    c. Can't argue with that
    d. Wow, you know, I can feel it too!

15. Eleventh-century monk St. Malachy recorded a prophecy of the history of the popes by writing a series of
    a. cryptic mottos for each
    b. dirty limericks for each
    c. funny rebuses for each
    d. bubble-gum cards for each

16. America's most famous prophet, Edgar Cayce, was known for making his psychic predictions in
    a. his sleep
    b. his wife's lingerie
    c. a high-pitched, sort of Chinese accent
    d. total disregard for the lack of accuracy among his previous prophecies

17. Nostradamus correctly predicted all of the following except
    a. Napoleon's defeat at Waterloo
    b. Hitler's invasion of France
    c. the assassination of John F. Kennedy
    d. the verdict in the O. J. Simpson trial

18. The ancient calendar of the Mayans is important for us today because
    a. it runs out in the year 2012
    b. a new pocket edition is being prepared by Hallmark
    c. it adds an important element of multiculturalism to telling time
    d. it sure didn't do them a lot of good

19. The <u>Harmonic Convergence</u> is
    a. the physical alignment of a number of planets with
       the sun, causing profound gravitational reactions,
       energy releases, and earth changes
    b. an advanced position described in the <u>Kama Sutra</u>
    c. a particularly difficult method of playing the har-
       monica
    d. a fancy name for a barbershop quartet convention

20. It is speculated that the continent of Atlantis was destroyed and sank in the ocean due to
    a. its abuse of crystal energy and disruption of the
       balance of nature
    b. the aloofness of its cultural elite
    c. shad-smoking among its teenagers
    d. gangsta rap

21. Which of the following characters does <u>not</u> appear in
the Book of Revelation?
    a. the Beast
    b. the False Prophet
    c. the Dragon
    d. the Rifleman

22. As sightings of UFOs have increased in recent years, it
has been speculated that aliens have been visiting us to
    a. help us usher in a new era of global consciousness
    b. discuss possible new sites for Wal-Mart
    c. protest their unfair depiction in <u>Mars Attacks!</u>
    d. tape Must See TV

23. Within the passageways of the Great Pyramid of Cheops,
researchers have discovered
    a. a physical chronology of the major events in world
       history
    b. the Pharaoh's secret stash of adult hieroglyphics
    c. blood planted by the Los Angeles Police Department
    d. a new Starbucks

24. According to surveys, most Americans will be spending
New Year's Eve 1999
    a. making elaborate resolutions to neglect in the next
       century
    b. being overserved
    c. shooting off handguns
    d. wondering how old Dick Clark really is

SCORE

Score? Who cares about the score? What do you think this
is, Reader's Digest? Quit trying to show how smart you are.
We're talking about the apocalypse here! If you want to impress people with your ready grasp of trivial knowledge, go
on Jeopardy! If you want to know how and when the world is
going to end, read on.

A.D. 999

Peasants and Monks Shout, "Give Up da Funk!"

A S THE YEAR 2000 bears down upon us, we naturally look for precedents in human history for clues as to how we might conduct ourselves. As we cross this momentous threshold, will we rise to the occasion with honest reflection on our past and renewed enthusiasm for the future, or will all hell break loose? For purposes of argument (as well as book sales), we must certainly predict the latter.

While political revolutions, labor riots, and NBA championships may hint at the kinds of upheaval in store for us, they are all incomplete comparisons. These events lack the element of transformation, the feeling of anxiety, the cosmic weight, the divine imprimatur. Only once before has mankind experienced such a tumultuous transition period and lived to tell the tale (sorry, all you baby boomers, I'm not talking about the Summer of Love).❡

In the year 999 A.D., a catastrophic transformation of the earth was awaited by everyone, or at least by those who counted their years since the birth of Jesus, and those who weren't cut off by geography, language, or quarantine from the main centers of culture (which in Europe were few and far between, anyway). With the expected Second Coming of Christ, God's grand experiment on earth was about to fold its tents permanently. So said every priest, theologian, soothsayer, mathematician, and prognosticator worth his salt.

The projected finale differed depending on location. In northern lands, the Germanic tribes believed the world would end in fire, and that God would have the

❡To experience the anticipation and dread felt by the people of 999, I spent many weekends last summer at King Canute's Renaissance Fayre in La Porte, Indiana. While the atmosphere was only partially accurate in a historical sense, I did gain many insights during long conversations with Myrick the Mud Eater and Pippin the Leper. I tip my pointed cap to these two generous people and their contributions to modern eschatological scholarship.

sense and common courtesy to destroy their countries first. Around the Mediterranean basin, the faithful believed the end would erupt from a mighty blast of Gabriel's trumpet, and would happen soon enough to spare them another winter season of pushy German tourists.

Soon, history's ultimate TGIF party commenced. Farmers didn't bother to plant crops for next year, since next year would never come. Barons and landlords gave away their estates, wishing to be unburdened by material goods when Jesus returned to claim his worldly kingdom. Peasants and serfs eagerly accepted the donation of these properties, presuming that the Son of God would be generous enough to cut some slack for the little guy. Infideli-

If 9 Was 6 ...

Some commentators have pointed out the significance of the inverse of the year 999, that is, 666—the number of the Beast in the Book of Revelation. This certainly would have added to the hysteria back then, had not the vast majority of the populace been so dog-stupid and the literate minority still using Roman numerals instead of Arabic. Instead of the year 999 gracefully turning over in the celestial odometer to 1000, for the learned in Europe the lumbering year CMXCIX crashed and the year M rose from the wreckage. While a large M may have significance for certain globe-girdling hamburger companies (and may yet in the year MM), this impact was lost on the medieval mind.

Meanwhile, the inverse of CMXCIX is actually XIOXWO, the significance of which is still being debated.

ties were forgiven, debts absolved, grievances settled, feuds resolved.

Everyday life in the tenth century was usually dangerous, chaotic, and unjust, but now even these certainties were swept away. Merchants closed up shop or simply gave their wares away (although there's no evidence of any special "End of the World" sales, such as we are likely to endure in our time). Farmers freed their animals, perhaps fearing that Christ had planted spies in the barnyard. These critters freely roamed the countryside, adding to the end-times confusion in a lighthearted, wacky manner.

Pilgrims marched off to the Holy Land for a choice seat for the end of the world; presumably, as in church, God would notice those seated in the front rows first. Both noble and peasant made this grand journey, abandoning their old stations in life for a greater camaraderie in the face of impending annihilation. While the question of who got to ride to Jerusalem and who had to walk has been lost in time, we can assume that Christian generosity prevailed unless one pilgrim was much larger than another. Because one's time was short and sins so many, whips and scourges were a part of everyone's travel kit. The first thought to come to the 20th-century mind might be, "What a great idea—commemorative souvenir scourges! Make 'em big enough and you can even sell advertising on 'em!" Unfortunately, such promotional ideas were alien to medieval thinking. The picture shown above, in fact, has proven to be nothing more than an artful forgery.

Of course, like every big bender, this millennial celebration had its dark side as well. Churches were desecrated with orgies and destroyed by riots. Penitents flogging themselves left trails of blood through the streets, and some sinners decided not to wait for God's judgment and ended their own lives instead. Buildings were left to crumble and crops left to rot in the fields, as serf and merchant alike reorganized their priorities in anticipation of the end.

Rivers swelled with floods greater than anyone had ever seen. Earthquakes split the ground and swallowed up whole cities. Epidemics swept through the countryside that put the plagues of Egypt to shame. The sun appeared twice in the sky. Fire and rock rained from heaven. Poodles walked on their hind legs and taught themselves to play the banjo.❦ These terrors continued throughout the last days, and as people gathered in churches and town squares on the night of December 31, 999, they turned their faces heavenward, expecting a show to end all shows.

Slowly, ominously, the clocks in the towers chimed twelve. Then, silence. Somebody coughed. As if possessed of one mind, the first thought of the faithful assembled was, "Y'know, I never *did* trust that clock."

No snooze button on this model.

The arrival of the new year saw no horns, no confetti, no furtive kisses with sexy neighbors—just the knowledge that the Almighty had somehow granted the world a reprieve. The party held after this realization has yet to be surpassed in joy, fervor, or alcohol consumption.

Or something like that. Or not.

❦Just kidding. Banjos hadn't even been invented yet.

Historians are now debating whether any of this up-heaval actually happened, since none of the era's official records mention anything out of the ordinary, aside from a French peasant who claimed to be possessed by a swarm of bees. There is even evidence that Gibbon and other historians invented these tales of chaos to highlight the ignorance of the Dark Agers. (Talk about some inse-cure intellectuals.)

Other practical questions arise concerning these ac-counts. Could, for example, the faithful watch the clock in the church steeple tick off to midnight if the first me-chanical clocks weren't invented until the late 13th cen-tury? And which New Year's Eve would people be celebrating, anyway? In Rome, the New Year began on December 25, but in Florence it started on March 25, the Feast of the Annunciation. Venice, just to be differ-ent, chose March 1, while France celebrated on Easter, and England could choose among Christmas, the Feast of the Circumcision (January 1), and Lady Day (March 25, some 900 years before Billie Holiday's birth). In the Byzantine world, September 1 or 24 served as the begin-ning of the New Year, while Armenia celebrated the New Year on July 9. This wide variety of choices would seem to make it easier to hit all the New Year's parties; if

One catastrophe chronicled in the art of the day was an invasion of unearthly steamrollers. (Steamroller portion not shown.)

Christ had already returned before a certain date, however, would one need to send regrets to the host?

It is not my intention to split hairs on whether or not hordes of Roman Catholics traveled thousands of miles to Jerusalem or liberated their chickens or decided to commit mass suicide in the year 999. If none of these events are recorded in the annals of that time, I'm sure there is some logical explanation, like a universal church conspiracy. The point in discussing this first millennial passing, as with so much else in this book, is not whether it is true. The point is to answer the question "How can I use this information to get ready for the *real* end of the world, which is certainly breathing down our necks right now?"

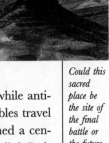

Could this sacred place be the site of the final battle or the future home of Trump Temple?

First off, the pilgrimage to the Holy Land, while anticlimactic in outcome, did give the European nobles travel experience for the Crusades, which were launched a century later after the indiscretions of the "Mad Caliph," al-Hakim, which included (ironically) banning Christian pilgrimages to the Holy Land. Those decades saw horrendous bloodshed and swapping insults of "infidel," as it looked like God couldn't make up his mind which side was his favorite. While the Middle East has been claimed by three of the world's major religions as holy and their own, after centuries of contention no clear winner has emerged. According to some modern commentators, we are about to witness Armageddon—the final battle between good and evil—near the Israeli town of Megiddo. Why would a holy land be so plagued by violence and pain? My guess is God may have consecrated this region just because he likes a good fight and the sight lines are generally unobstructed.

One lesson we can take from this is that any prepa-

Did doomsday comets strike fear into superstitious medieval hearts, or is this evidence of early airplane banner advertising? (Actual unretouched woodcut.)

ration for the millennium, no matter how costly or ludicrous, may bring unforeseen benefits later. If, for example, you work ceaselessly to connect like-minded people around the world electronically so that the critical mass of their positive mental energies can inaugurate a new era of enlightened consciousness, at the very least you'll improve your computer skills.

A second lesson to consider: It seems very unlikely, at this stage of human evolution, that wealthy landowners will be giving away large amounts of property. No real benefits exist under current tax laws, and possible liability issues remain murky. If indeed it does happen, it will likely be to high-profile charities so donors can reap the maximum publicity possible. Those of you who keep sending Sylvester Stallone apocalyptic pamphlets and hanging around Planet Hollywood hoping he'll mend his ways and toss you the keys to his condo in Aspen are wasting your time.

The final lesson we can take from the tribulations of our medieval brothers and sisters is that you have to make your own apocalypse. As with gardening and volunteer work, the more you put into your millennial vision, the more you'll get out of it. You might think that

999 vs. Today:
Coincidence or What?

Median life expectancy: 17	Median emotional age: 17
An ignorant, illiterate population relies on privileged, self-serving demagogues to interpret the world around them	24-hour talk radio
Traveling mountebanks, magicians, and swindlers	Economists, pollsters, and televangelists
Tubercular peasants dressed in rags and covered with mud, filth, and grime	Models in Details magazine
The faithful venerate fingers, thigh bones, and other relics of the saints	The Beatles Anthology, Vol. III
People live in rickety huts and lean-tos, constantly fearful of attack	People live in 10-room houses in gated communities, constantly fearful of attack
Vikings invade settlements, plunder populations, and destroy local European culture	The world is overrun by satellite TV and McDonald's

your personal contribution won't bring about the end of the world, but don't sell yourself short. You'd be surprised what you can accomplish with a little hard work, a positive attitude, and homemade packets of nerve gas.

Moreover, looking back a thousand years ago, we can see another constant for our race: There's nothing like a catastrophe to give people a feeling of connectedness and common purpose. Witness the success of movies like *Independence Day*. In a medieval vein, imagine Bill Pullman as a young bishop exhorting the rabble that the end is near, Jeff Goldblum as the soothsayer who has determined the exact date and hour, and Will Smith as the spunky peasant who makes good in the topsy-turvy world of 999 A.D. How's *that* for the feel-good event of the first millennium?

Prophecy

The Heavy Hitters

THE MAN
WHO SAW
TOMORROW

WRITING ABOUT THE FUTURE without mentioning Nostradamus would be like writing about art without mentioning LeRoy Neiman.

He is the most famous, the most quoted, the most widely analyzed and apparently the most successful prophet in modern history. He foresaw, among other events, the Great London Fire of 1666, the French Revolution, the fall of the Romanovs, World War II (though not World War I), and the atomic bomb. Believers in his prophecies range from Catherine de Médicis and Elizabeth I to Orson Welles and Dudley Moore. He is, according to one commentator, the "Wayne Gretzky of the world of prophecy."

He was trained as a physician in 16th-century France, an era when most learned men studied astronomy and astrology along with general science (possibly because courses in creative writing and social psychology weren't available even on the graduate level). Also, despite the best efforts of the Inquisition, belief in the occult was fairly common. On the surface, Nostradamus was your average postmedieval doctor/alchemist/future visionary. What sets Nostradamus apart from seers of his time and ours is the power of his predictions. So great is his influence and so accurate his visions that he has been translated and reprinted continually since his first publication. (The only other book that can claim such popularity is the Bible.) And with the rapid unfolding of world events, new translations and interpretations of his puzzling poems will keep publishers jumping for years.

(Many people don't know that Nostradamus also made an important mark as a cosmetician and chef. His *Treatise on Makeup* contained many recipes for beauty creams of all sorts, including one for a "rejuvenating pomade" made of coral, leaf gold, and lapis lazuli. His specialty as a chef was a "quince jelly, of a sovereign beauty, goodness, taste and excellence proper to be presented to a king." So, for a true picture of the greatness of the man, imagine combining parts of Sydney Omarr, La Toya Jackson and her psychic hotline, Coco Chanel and Mrs. Smuckers, plus a little Dr. Quinn, Medicine Woman.)

A strange and magical combination.

Michel de Nostredame was born in 1503 in Provence to a middle-class family of recently Christianized Jews. He was a bright child, schooled by his grandfathers in astrology and history (and mystic sciences such as the Hebrew Kabbalah❡ and alchemy, according to

❡The Kabbalah was a mystical branch of Judaic studies that sought to unlock the hidden meanings in each word and letter of the Old Testament. For the hidden meanings of the previous sentence, watch for my next book, *Kabbalah: What Did You Mean by That, Bubbe?*, in bookstores soon.

some), and later went to study medicine. But like so many people of his ethnic background, he felt torn between a comfortable income as a doctor and the bright lights and adulation of stardom. We still see people struggling with this dilemma in community theater groups everywhere.

He chose to work in medicine and, luckily for Nostradamus, the years following 1525 were good ones for the plague in southern France. He gained a wide reputation for his skills and bravery in treating the horrid affliction. According to some, he gathered rose petals for making vitamin C lozenges for his patients and cured a great many sufferers. The fact that rose petals contain no vitamin C (although rose hips do), or that vitamins might prevent someone from catching the plague but could never cure it, is beside the point when we try to measure the greatness of the man or the accuracy of his modern interpreters.

His medical work, unfortunately, kept him away from home for great lengths of time, and his wife and two young children succumbed to the dread disease he was busy combating. That no psychic premonition of their deaths came to the most gifted seer of all time may be curious, but there is probably a simple explanation. Maybe he didn't check his psychic messages that day. He was a busy man, hey! But this disaster did nothing for his professional reputation.

Heartbroken, Nostradamus left his home in Agen and wandered Europe for a decade, practicing medicine here and there and consulting with astrologers and others in the mystic arts. Some sources say his divinatory powers increased greatly during this period and he sometimes made predictions of the future to amuse friends at gatherings, a popular pastime of sixth-grade slumber parties even today. He eventually settled again in Salon, where he married a wealthy widow. He practiced medicine by day and prognosticated by night. The upstairs room of his house was converted into a secret study. It was there that Nostradamus saw the future (or a reasonable facsimile thereof).

His methods were borrowed from ancient sources. By the light of a single candle, Nostradamus sat before a shallow brass basin of water and aromatic oils (perhaps the cosmetician in him knew this would also be good for his pores). He emptied his mind to allow the spirits of prophecy to fill it. He next dipped a wand into the water and touched it to the hem of his robe and to his feet. Then, in the rising mists of the basin, the show would begin.

Imagine what Nostradamus could have seen if he had had better light.

Nostradamus recorded his prophetic visions in quatrains. The first volume of these, *Centuries*, was published in 1555. Despite its lack of dessert recipes, the book gained Nostradamus fame among the nobility and the upper crust. These were powerful friends he sorely needed, since the Inquisition was rolling merrily along at this time, and church leaders did not look kindly on soothsayers and visionaries (except, of course, their own). A successful magician, especially one of Nostradamus's ethnic background, would provide enough work for a squad of ecclesiastical judges, jailers, confessional engineers, and disembowelment specialists. Nostradamus's challenge was thus to publish his prophecies and at the same time make them nearly impossible to understand.

Nostradamus hid the true meaning of his visions in the poems ingeniously—so ingeniously, in fact, that after 400 years we are still trying to decipher them. In her latest book, *The Final Prophecies of Nostradamus*, noted expert Erika Cheetham admits that 367 of the 941 quatrains in *Centuries* are so ambiguous that they make no sense at the present time.❜ (She refers to them cryptically as "unsuccessful" or "failed" quatrains.) But just wait and see if someone doesn't come up with an accurate interpretation (or dozens!) for each in the future.

Nostradamus obscured his meanings in several ways—word games, anagrams, puns, symbolic language, and classical allusions among them. He also arranged his poems in random order, so finding actual dates and historical sequences is difficult. A bit of an intellectual show-off, he wrote *Centuries* in a mixture of French, Italian, Provençal, Latin, and Greek, but only a *Homo stultissimus* would swallow such jejune legerdemain *à bouche ouverte, non?* Whether he also wrote in Pig Latin, bebop lingo, or Ubby-Dubby depends on the ingenuity of the interpreter and the credulity of the reader. But that *Nostradamus* perfectly saw into the future, there can be no doubt.

Stud Oarsman

Take, for example, the hidden messages in the following quatrain:

> Beasts mad with hunger will
> swim across rivers,
>   The greater part of the
> battlefield will be against
> Hister.
>   He will drag the great one in
> a cage of iron,
>   When the child of Germany
> observes no law.

❜Another expert, John Hogue, puts it this way: "Of his known 1,082 quatrains, over 800 are little more than augury-babble. . . . In my opinion, many of the incomprehensible quatrains are accurate chronicles of events which might have been, if history had taken a different turn—predictions for a parallel universe, in fact." Can't argue with that.

Which Three Brothers?

One of the sure signs of the coming of the apocalypse, according to Nostradamus, will be the death of an influential trio of "three beautiful children." Some think this is a very straightforward reference to the Kennedy brothers, but is it really? Consider:

John, Robert, and Ted Kennedy—Only two are dead, although the third one drifts in and out of consciousness.

Their Royal Highnesses, Charles, Andrew, and Edward—Calling them beautiful is a stretch, even for Nostradamus.

Matty, Felipe, and Jesus Alou—Baseball references are notoriously absent elsewhere in Centuries.

Manny, Moe, and Jack—The Pep Boys are merely fictional pitchmen.

Moe, Curly, and Shemp Howard—While all are dead, the omission of key Stooge Larry Fine is too stark to remain unexplained.

The only obvious choice left is the Marx Brothers (minus Zeppo, of course), whose surname calls us back to Karl Marx and the Communist revolution, which brings up issues too complicated to go into in a sidebar like this.

Could the name *Hister* be any more clearly a reference to Adolf Hitler?[†] By switching the *s* and *t* in Hister, and then stretching the *s* taut into a straight line, you come up with the famous Nazi's name. And the rest of the quatrain, of course, refers to World War II—at least, the mention of Germany does.

Was he or wasn't he?

Hister, it may not surprise you, was an avid fan of Nostradamus, as were Propaganda Minister Joseph Goebbels and other prominent goosesteppers. In fact, their propaganda machine enlisted astrologers at gunpoint to devise pro-Nazi translations of Nostradamus, then had them printed and air-dropped over France. (Whether Der Führer knew he himself was prominently featured in the poems is not recorded.) Taking a stand against such silliness, the British had their own anti-Axis versions printed up and distributed. (And you think *you're* worried about how your tax money is spent?) When America entered the war, Hollywood newsreels proclaimed that Nostradamus had predicted victory for the Allies. So there, Mr. Master Race. Nostradamus was right all along!

So what does Nostradamus have to say about the end of the world? Plenty, as long as you read it right. The times leading up to the millennium will be filled with wars, plagues, natural disasters, and famine. And it is truly difficult, from our personal, late-20th-century perspective, to imagine a world more troubled than our own. Specific historic events that Nostradamus foresaw include the Kennedy assassinations, the collapse of the Soviet Union, the death of Pope John Paul I, the war in Yugoslavia, the

[†] Actually, it could. Hister was the name the ancient Romans gave the River Danube. This was known to Nostradamus, because he uses it elsewhere to refer to that river. But here it has a double meaning, if you rearrange the letters and misspell it. Clever, huh?

Gulf War, and the rise of Saddam Hussein. Then, in a rare use of a specific date, Nostradamus predicts

> In the year 1999, and seven months
> From the sky will come the great King of Terror.
> He will bring to life the great King of the Mongols.
> Before and after, Mars reigns happily.

The king of the Mongols might be Genghis Khan, or another ruler from that part of the world. Keep your eye on Outer Mongolia for further developments.

Since Mars, the god of war, "reigns happily" before and after, we might assume that the world will not end abruptly. This may be the start of massive unrest, the "Tribulation" anticipated by pre-millenarian Christians today. Mars is also the god of spiritual transformation, so many New Agers believe this predicts mass enlightenment for the planet. Mars is also a candy company, producers of M&Ms and Zag-Nut bars, so stockholders may want to bolster their portfolios as this natural promotional tie-in approaches.

What Khan go wrong next?

Roast Us? Damn! ——*Nostradamus* envisioned three "Antichrists" who would arise and wreak havoc on mankind. The first two were Napoleon and Hister. We're still guessing about the identity of the third, although it seems likely he has already started his work and is a native of the Middle East. If you want to get astrological about it, he was born under three "water signs" (insert your own tavern joke here). He will also wear a blue turban, so be on the lookout. His turn-ons, turn-offs, and favorite movies are still being debated, but most of his high school classmates described him as "serious."

With the arrival of the Antichrist will come a 27-year war, according to Nostradamus, with "blood, human bodies, water and red hail covering the earth." The Antichrist will install an antipope in the Vatican and declare a new Holy Roman Empire. This will last a mere seven months, after which both will be killed and their supporters axed. Much nastiness will ensue, but eventually a reign of Saturn or Age of Gold will arrive, and Satan will be powerless for 1,000 years.

Or something like that. Or not.

Anyway, for our purposes, the intent is clear: The end of the world will begin sometime in July 1999, and the upheavals will last for an unspecified period of time. Curiously, this doesn't stop our mystic man from going on: He writes to his son César that the world will really end in 3797 A.D., and elsewhere states (through descriptions of rare celestial alignments) that the world will really, really end 42 years after *that*. Is this thoroughness or thoughtlessness? Was Nostradamus hedging his bets? We'll have to leave this question for Nostradamians to ponder for the next 2,000 years.

JULY 1999

SUN	MON	TUES	WED	THURS	FRI	SAT
1	2	3	4	5	6	7
8	9	10	11	12	?	14
15	16	17	18	19	20	21
22	23	24	25	26	27	28
29	30	31				

Keep your schedule clear.

One glaring omission in Nostradamus's writing still confuses his champions and critics, however: For all his proven and speculated abilities, not one of his predictions foresaw the cataclysm of the Cleveland Browns moving to Baltimore.

Cap'n NOSTY

HEY KIDS! IT'S **FUN** TO PREDICT THE FUTURE!

ANAGRAM FUN!

REARRANGE THE JUMBLED WORDS TO MAKE REAL NAMES. THEN, ARRANGE THE LETTERS IN THE BOXES TO ANSWER THE RIDDLE.

EDCUDE = N Ⓐ POLE Ⓞ N

KLCYU = ST Ⓐ LI N

ENVIX = KE NNE Ⓓ Y

LECAB = Ⓨ ELTS Ⓘ N

EVERY MORNING, HE'S UP BEFORE YOU ARE!

THE AYATOLLAH

MATCHING

DRAW A LINE BETWEEN THE PICTURE AND THE THING IT REPRESENTS!

THE PAPACY

ENGLAND

FLU EPIDEMICS

A WHALE

TELL THE FUTURE!

OH **HO!** WHAT DOES THE FUTURE HOLD FOR *THIS* LITTLE SHAVER?

COOKIES

ANSWER: AFTER THE PRIVANCES ARE BURNED, THE ASS DRIVERS WILL BE FORCED TO CHANGE INTO DIFFERENT CLOTHING. THOSE OF SATURN, BURNED BY THE MILKERS, BUT THE GREATER PART EXCEPTED, IT WILL NOT BE RECOVERED.

MIRROR MESSAGE

HOLD UP TO A MIRROR TO SEE TODAY'S SECRET MESSAGE!

GARNER IS THE BEAST

THE DOPE ON THE POPES

MÁEL MÁEDOC ÚA MORGAIR was an 11th-century Irish bishop credited with introducing the Roman liturgy to the Emerald Isle. He was reputed to have the powers of healing, levitation, and clairvoyance, and on the strength of his miracles, Máel Máedoc Úa Morgair was (luckily for our tongues) made St. Malachy a few years after his death, the first Irish native to be canonized. As befits a son of the Old Sod, he had an abiding sense of doom, which has earned him a place in the annals of prophecy.

As the story opens, our intrepid saint was on his way to an audience with Pope Innocent II. When St. Malachy came within view of the seven hills of Rome, he fell off his donkey and went into an ecstatic trance, in which he beheld a procession of all the popes from his own time until the demise of the papacy. After he emerged from this wonderful vision, he recorded a brief motto describing each of the popes he had seen. Malachy later presented this list as a gift to Innocent II, although history does not record his reaction (probably somewhere between "Thank Baal! I'm not the last one" and "I guess building that addition on the south wing is a better idea than I thought"). With all that out of the way, the Pope and the saint got down to discussing important things, like financing more Crusades with bingo money.

Prophetic papal hit parades apparently being run-of-the-mill around the Vatican, Malachy's *Prophetia de Futuribus Pontificibus Romanis* was misplaced in papal archives until 1595, when it was published by a Benedictine monk. The *Prophetia* contained thumbnail sketches of 112 popes, beginning with Innocent's successor, Celestine II (no relation to *The Celestine Prophecy*). While some cynics have pointed out that the descriptions of the popes are incredibly accurate for those reigning before 1595 and quite logically contorted for those since then, I prefer to think of this as merely coincidence. What is more important about St. Malachy's vision is something that has become apparent only in this century: The last Holy Father will be set on the throne around the year 2000. The popes are on the ropes, and so are we all.

Sly Ham Act

The church's official opinion is that this prophetic list is a forgery. Ignoring the opinion of their scientific "experts," however, will lead us down a more interesting and fruitful path. For each pope, Malachy's mottoes describe something idiosyncratic—a coat of arms, a family name, a birthplace, previous church positions, or a papal reign (no relation to the album *Purple Rain*, by the Artist Formerly Known as Prince). Some examples:

B	I	N	G	O
III	XVI	XXII	XLVI	LXI
V	XIX	XXXV	XLIX	LXIV
VIII	XXIII	☠	LII	LXIX
XI	XXVI	XL	LVII	LXXI
XIV	XXIX	XLIII	LIX	LXXIV

In excelsis Bingo.

No. 46, Boniface IX . . . . "Wears pointy hat"
No. 72, Gregory XIII . . . "Likes Italian food"
No. 89, Clement XI . . . . "No sex, please"
No. 99, Pius VIII . . . . "Sure knows his Latin"

Well, not really, but you get the idea. At first glance, this would appear to be an interesting but trivial prophecy—the equivalent of reading descriptions in a high school yearbook ("Pope with the Sunniest Smile," "Pope Most Likely to Succeed," "Homecoming Pope," etc.). But as we mentioned, Malachy's list contains 112 popes, and it has to run out sometime. Luckily for us, that sometime is very soon.

The papacy may end early in the 21st century, leaving unresolved the critical question, Who will inherit those fabulous hats?

The predictions for the 20th-century popes are stunningly accurate. The motto for Pius XI, who cut a deal with Mussolini and was given the area of Vatican City in return, was "Fides Intrepida"—"Start printing postage stamps."❢

Paul VI, who issued the papal encyclical condemning artificial birth control, had as a motto "Flos Florum"—"Flower of flowers," a nicely poetic description of the beauty of a woman in her third trimester.

The tragic figure of John Paul I in some ways stands as a personification of the twilight of the papacy. After less than a month in office, he died of a heart attack, although some believe he was murdered by conservative cardinals because of the radical church reforms he was suddenly (and uncharacteristically) going to announce. On Malachy's list, John Paul I had as a motto, "De Medietate Lunae"—"Of the half moon"—which has a number of connotations:

❧ He was born in the Italian province of Belluno, "beautiful moon."

❢The literal Latin translation is "intrepid faith," but because of Pius's toadying to Il Duce—at one time he gushed, "Benito Mussolini is . . . a gift of Providence, a man free from the prejudices of the politicians of the liberal school"—we are forced to be more creative in our interpretation.

꩜ He was elected on the first day of the last quarter of the moon, and died on the last day of the first quarter—both times when the moon is a perfect half-disk in the sky.

꩜ His pre-pope name, Albino Luciani, means "white light," just like we get from the moon!

꩜ One of his favorite songs was Dean Martin's "That's Amore," which begins, "When the moon hits your eye like a big pizza pie . . . "

Some have interpreted his motto as "Cup of coffee" or "Don't bother to unpack," but these are obviously self-serving mistranslations.

His successor, John Paul II, has as a motto "De Laboris Solis." This does not mean "Copycat name" or "Owns glass-top convertible," but rather "From the labor of the sun." The former Karol Wojtyla certainly works hard. He is from Kraków, where many years earlier Copernicus toiled to prove his theory about the earth revolving around the sun (which ironically got him booted from the Catholic church). And the pun on sun/Son (Jesus) only underscores Malachy's prophetic skill, as he was able to employ double-meaning wordplay in a modern language that existed in a very different form 800 years ago (and wasn't even remotely similar to his native Gaelic)!

Following today's pope are just two more mottoes. Some debate exists as to whether they might not be the same person. The next pope's motto is "Gloria Olivae"—"The glory of the olive." Does this mean the pope will be of the Benedictine (or Olivetan) order? Will he come from the Middle East, famous for its olives? Will he have a background in bartending?

After the glory of the olive comes the end of St. Malachy's prophecy. No motto is given for this last pope, only the following prediction:

In the final persecution, the seat of the Holy Roman Church will be occupied by Peter the Roman, who will feed the flock through many tribulations: after which the city of seven hills will be destroyed, and the formidable Judge shall judge his people. The end.

The city of the seven hills is, of course, Rome. The flock is the members of the church. Peter the Roman is apparently some Italian fellow named Peter. Once all these are in place, the Second Coming and God's final judgment will occur.

For scholarship's sake, I feel the need to point out a glitch in St. Malachy's work. While he did foresee the schism that resulted in the election of four antipopes in the 12th century (to all of whom he gave mottoes), he failed to include Innocent III, who reigned in 1179–80. He also failed to include Benedict XIV, the counter-antipope (or "hidden" pope) of 1425, whose legitimacy is suspect and story too confusing to retell here. If these two individuals are counted in the roster, it would mean that we are currently on the 112th and final pope. It would also mean Kraków's Karol Wojtyla, John Paul II, is actually Peter of Rome, and that every pope since 1425 needs to have his motto revamped or reinterpreted. None of this, however, need detract from our acceptance of *St. Malachy's* prophecy. After all, when he fell off his donkey, he was probably soused.

Scaly Math

SIZE 5¼

THE HABERDASHER WHO CRIED WOLF

ZEALOTRY ENJOYED a golden era in the late 19th century, with robber barons, temperance workers, and doomsday prophets vying for headlines. One of the most prominent of the latter was Charles Taze Russell, a Pennsylvania haberdasher who founded the Jehovah's Witnesses.

Since the group's establishment in 1884, the end of the world and the Second Coming of Christ have been a cornerstone of the Jehovah's Witnesses (officially known as the Watchtower Bible and Tract Society). In fact, in this century alone, the Society has officially predicted the end at least five times. The unofficial count (through rumors, speculation, and the like) is pretty impressive as well. In fact, the *Watchtower* magazine, the official Society organ, has stated that the end is coming "soon" in every single issue ever printed since its beginning in 1879—a pretty clever way to get subscribers to renew, when you think about it.

From the start, when Russell began preaching something he called the "Millennial Dawn," he said Jesus had returned to earth invisibly in 1874 to set up his kingdom. Jesus would wait 40 years, through the "Gentile times" (as described in Luke 21:24), and in 1914 would judge humanity and punish the wicked. By Russell's estimation, October 2 would be the destruction date for the "Gentile nations." On this day, chosen Witnesses would be taken to heaven, while Christ's millennial reign on earth would begin.

Jest Who Vanishes?

So did this happen? Hard to say. According to one *Jehovah's Witness* leader, Russell bounded down the stairs to breakfast on the morning of October 2, "briskly clapped his hands and happily announced: 'The Gentile times have ended.'" Yet the milkman still came that day, the buses still ran, and worldly kingdoms had failed to topple. Setting the standard for ideological gymnastics that the group carries on to this day, Russell explained that Christ had indeed defeated Satan and established his Kingdom—only he had done it in the outermost heavens, where we mortals couldn't see it. Worldly kingdoms, while still around, were now invalid. Russell said the public had misinterpreted his prophecy, which hadn't stated *explicitly* that Christ would set up anything on earth. (Boy, you start telling people about the end of worldly kingdoms and Christ's return and they start jumping to all sorts of nutty conclusions!)

How long did Adam run single with his animal buddies before Eve worked her Rules-girl magic? The answer is an essential part of apocalyptic calculations.

Between 1914 and 1918, the Witnesses concocted their best-known prophetic slogan: "Millions now living will never die!" The Battle of Armageddon and the start of the millennium were close at hand, and would erupt before the last of a group of 144,000 specially appointed Witnesses died.❡ This "generation" would not die, according to Scripture, until the Second Coming took place. The actual definition of "generation" has caused some problems since then. The Society has recently stopped defining it as the physical lifespan of a human being and instead now considers it an era. This extends the imminence of the "end times" almost indefinitely, although once the last of the 144,000 dies, regular unanointed members will take over the Society leadership, which could wreak absolute havoc on their current record of apocalyptic accuracy.

Other years chosen by Witnesses for the Big One❡❡:

1918: When this year came and went, church leaders told their followers that the prediction was not wrong, only unapparent. Their official explanation was that Christ had entered God's celestial temple in order to cleanse it. God's poor housekeeping habits were news to many.

1925: The second president of the Witnesses, "Judge" Joseph Rutherford, stated that this was the beginning of the era touted by "Millions now living . . ." He also preached that the saints and prophets of the Old Testament would be resurrected, and used church money to

❡Eighty-three years later, it is believed a survey of that appointed group would fail to yield statistically significant data, or even enough for a hand of canasta.

❡❡Is it just me, or is the word *witnesses* taking on a slightly ironic tone by now?

build these returnees a huge mansion in San Diego. When nothing happened that year, the church lost three-quarters of its members. According to Frederick Franz, the Witnesses' fourth president, in a speech in 1975, Rutherford admitted "that he had made an ass of himself over 1925."

1941: Undaunted, "Judge" Rutherford stated that the outbreak of World War II was a sign that the end was near. Rutherford's own end was near, anyway, which might have caused great concern among some Witnesses (although relief for their public relations department).

Then, finally, enough horsing around: 1975 was really, really, *really* going to be it, said church leaders. Jehovah's Witnesses adhere to the popular "6,000 years and out" dogma. According to their math, Adam and Eve were created in 4026 B.C., so the 6,000 years were up in 1975.

When this prophecy again failed, many disappointed Witnesses left the church. The official explanation was that the length of Adam's bachelor days (i.e., the time between Adam's creation and Eve's) was unknown, so the 1975 choice was purely speculative. But Society members had no one to blame but themselves, according to Franz. "Do you know why nothing happened in 1975?" he asked an audience the following year. "It was because *you* expected something to happen." Christ, of course, explicitly warned that no one can know the hour of his return (Matthew 25:13 and elsewhere).

Of course, if we take Jesus's word as gospel, it would seem to negate the very foundations laid by *Rehearsals Cull Zest* — *Charles Taze Russell* when he established the Jehovah's Witnesses. But why quibble about history when there's so much to look forward to (constantly and as a part of church doctrine) in the future?

Clip and Hang

Most people learn about Jehovah's Witnesses doctrine through a screen door, at a time when they would rather be doing just about anything other than listening to an uninvited stranger in a cheap suit tell them about their impending damnation. So as a handy aid when they come a-knockin', just clip out the reference card below and hang it on your inside doorknob. You'll be glad you did.

WHAT TO DO IN CASE OF A JEHOVAH'S WITNESS

1. Open your front door, but keep your screen door shut.

2. Tell the person, "Yes, I'd love to hear about our impending annihilation, but I have something in the oven. Can you wait right here? I'll be back soon."

3. Shut the door and go about your business. A Witness who knows his church's doctrine will know that "soon" is a very elastic term.

4. Ignore any further knocking.

THE PROPHET SLEEPS TONIGHT

AMERICA'S OWN HOME-GROWN version of Nostradamus is the well-known "Sleeping Prophet," Edgar Cayce. This meek, unassuming farm boy, born in 1877 near Hopkinsville, Kentucky, dropped out of school in the seventh grade and grew up to become the most famous prophet and psychic of his time. Yet for all his mystic powers, he remained a simple country sort, a fundamentalist who read his Bible daily and taught Sunday school for most of his life. (Of course, he also believed in reincarnation—which, along with astral projection, channeling, and astrology, is not a big hit among fundamentalists today.) If Andy Griffith's Mayberry were ever to have a resident psychic, Cayce would fit the bill nicely.

Cayce's nickname is the "Sleeping Prophet," not because he knows when you've been sleeping and knows when you're awake. The tag describes his preferred method of tapping into the "Universal Consciousness." For his psychic readings he would lie down on a couch in

L

his office, loosen his clothing for comfort, and await the arrival of his "inner light," or connection with his channel. While in this light trance, he would dictate medical cures for the ill believers who sought his advice, give his opinions on current events and police cases,[*] and announce his visions for the future. Cayce held more than 14,000 of these sessions, all of which were transcribed and are kept carefully indexed by the Association for Research and Enlightenment, founded by Cayce devotees in 1931 in Virginia Beach, Virginia.

The diagnosis and cure of illness became Cayce's greatest area of renown. Believers traveled many miles for a personal interview with Cayce, followed by a diagnostic trance (certainly attractive to those who had lost their faith in modern medicine and those too shy to undress in front of strangers). Other sufferers, often with incurable diseases, wrote letters to Cayce describing their symptoms and imploring his help. Cayce's wife would read these letters to him while he was in one of his sleeplike trances, and Cayce would dictate a cure for the person to take. The remedies were natural and homeopathic —roots, bark, and berries boiled down into nauseating syrups. They were also rather ingeniously unorthodox, such as the osteopathic treatments he prescribed for people suffering from tuberculosis, epilepsy, and cancer. But such is the case with inspiration and psychic genius. He often described diseases and recommended treatments in terms that would only be known by highly educated doctors. Whether these treatments were proper, suitable, or effective is almost beside the point.

[*]Cayce lent his expertise to aid in the most famous criminal case of his era, the Lindbergh kidnapping, with the stipulation that he receive no publicity for it. This provision in itself showed great foresight, since just about every fact he predicted in the case proved incorrect. But that snafu, just like the Lindbergh baby himself, is neither here nor there.

Like any prophet worth his salt (or any other crystal), Cayce also had frequent visions of the times ahead. Among his more spectacular predictions were:

❧ The death of two American presidents while in office, a vision fulfilled by the deaths of Presidents Roosevelt and Kennedy. It is an especially bold prediction when you consider that, in the previous 100 years, only three American presidents had been assassinated and three others died in office.

❧ The beginning and end of both world wars. As a child, he saw a vision of flaming chariots rushing past his garden, a sure sign of World War I, which broke out suddenly some 30 years later.

❧ The resurfacing of the lost continent of Atlantis off the coast of the Bahamas, beginning in 1969. Although this event is tardy by 28 years and counting, we should allow our hopes great latitude here. To start with, think of the tourist possibilities! Tour boats filled with people dressed like bottle-nosed dolphins and Namor the Sub-Mariner would race out

Cayce pointed the way, and surely Kathie Lee will soon follow.

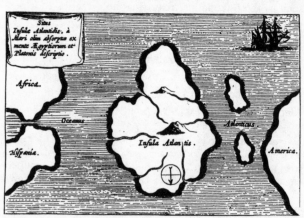

of Nassau morning, noon, and night. Pilgrims could walk the ancient, algae-strewn streets of this formerly mythical kingdom, munching fish sticks and calamari rings. It would make *Star Trek* conventions look like bridge night in Altoona.

Pole Shift: What Is It, and What Will Happen to All the Penguins?

One of the grandest and most efficiently destructive planetary catastrophes that may be on our horizons is a pole shift. This drastic relocation of the earth's axial poles—predicted by many to happen in May of 2001—would cause the loose mantle of the earth to slip around chaotically, causing massive earthquakes, floods, volcanoes, and address changes. The cause of all this shimmying is the polar ice caps, which some people insist are getting so big and heavy that they're making the earth wobble on its axis.

To test this theory at home, take a basketball and cover it first with a layer of chocolate syrup (representing molten magma), then with a layer of dirt (the earth's crust). Then pack snow and ice shavings on the top and bottom of the ball 3/4" to 1" thick. Finally, spin the ball on the tips of your fingers like a Harlem Globetrotter.

Did it make a mess? Are you covered with mud, ice, and chocolate? Man, you ain't seen nothin' yet.

All of this prophecy would be merely the ramblings of a self-deluded, spotlight-loving Walter Mitty with a messiah complex, promoted and protected by a group of blinkered devotees with too much time on their hands, were it not for the fact that, in a trance-induced reading in 1934, Cayce also foresaw a radical upheaval of the surface of the earth around the year 2000.

Accede Gave Yarns

According to *Edgar Evans Cayce*, the earth will be struck by a series of natural disasters in the 60-year period leading up to 2000, with an especially heavy concentration from 1958 to 1998. Earthquakes and volcanic eruptions will increase as the earth's mantle shifts and pitches. Especially important are volcanic eruptions of Mount Vesuvius in Italy and Mount Pelée in Martinique, which will trigger volcanic activity all over the earth. If (when!) these two peaks erupt, within three months massive earthquakes will devastate the "southern coast of California, particularly the areas between Salt Lake City and Southern Nevada," according to one British expert (an expert in prophecy, apparently, not geography).

The result of all this chaos will be a shift in the earth's poles, which will transform lands with frigid climates into tropical paradises. The United Nations should consider itself warned: This change will require huge airlifts of limbo records and sunblock to the sun-drenched islands of Scandinavia, and wool blankets and space heaters to Africa, India, and Southeast Asia. The ocean floors will rise and fall and the polar ice caps will melt, causing tidal waves and inundations on a massive scale. The results of these cataclysmic shocks are summarized in the following chart.

CAYCE'S PREDICTION	PREDICTABLE AFTERMATH
The Great Lakes will empty into the Mississippi River.	The bottom of Lake Michigan will yield many treasures, including shipwrecks, Chicago ballot boxes, and Jimmy Hoffa.
New York disappears into the ocean.	The ocean spits it right back up.
Land appears between Tierra del Fuego and Antarctica.	Britain and Argentina go to war over it.
New lands appear off the East Coast of America.	A vacant apartment is still impossible to find in Manhattan.
The safe lands will be "portions of what is now Ohio, Indiana and Illinois, and much of the southern portion of Canada and the eastern portion of Canada."	Dominance of Central Division teams in the World Series and the Super Bowl for the foreseeable future. Also, the ascendancy in national politics of the Quayle dynasty.
Open waters appear in the northern portion of Greenland.	None. Who gives a shit about Greenland?

Despite all this, according to Cayce, the earth and humankind will survive. In fact, these changes will herald the Second Coming of Christ and are warnings to us to begin construction of the New Jerusalem:

> To those then, that are come into the new life, the new under-standing — the new regeneration, there is then the new Jerusalem — not as a place, alone, but as a condition, as an experience of the soul.

If you thought that all the talk about "experiences of the soul," "regeneration," and a "new age" were merely modern brain flatulence, guess again. Cayce had already announced the arrival of the New Age in 1932. He also described how he would be reincarnated in 1998, as a "possible liberator of the world," and again in 2100, when he would visit the sites of all his previous incarnations with a group of long-haired scientists in a big, silver, cigar-shaped flying ship.

With his marvelous record, who can doubt that he will be proven right again?

Dear Diary

My Own Little Prophecy Journal

AFTER RESEARCHING HISTORY'S illustrious seers for this book, I began to feel very much a rookie on the subject of soothsaying. Not to put too fancy a spin on it, I became downright envious of these people's gifts at foretelling the future (their poor track record for the end of the world notwithstanding). I know what you're thinking—envy is a negative emotion and an impediment to my growth as a human being and as an occupant of this planet—but I couldn't stop thinking, "Who do these clowns think they are, anyway?" Finally, I decided to purge these resentful feelings by trying my own hand at prophecy. It couldn't hurt. Who knows (literally)? I might even have an untapped psychic gift.

What would you think if I sang out of tune? Would you box up and throw dirt on me?

I must admit I have never felt any particular inclination or affinity for this. At sleepovers, for example, I never could get a Ouija board to work properly, because of its lack of punctuation marks and limitations in conveying irony. Likewise, after hours of absorbing the music and the album art for *Sgt. Pepper,* I kept getting the impression that the deceased Beatle was Ringo (although his career has been dead for years, I still don't think it counts). But it's been said that everyone has a little psychic inside him itching to get out (at least the little internal psychic sends some message like this telepathically), so I decided to try my hand at a few different methods of prognostication to see which ones would strike a chord within me.

TEA-LEAF READING

The reading of tea leaves, technically known as *tasseography*, is one of the oldest methods of divining the future. Some connoisseurs have their own preferences for the best teas to use, as well as the best china, seed cakes, and finger sandwiches, but nearly all say that broadleaf jasmine tea is one of the best and most

Puzzling?
Perplexing?
Darjeeling?

reliable. It also conjures up images of far-away lands, foreign intrigues, and squalid opium dens, so the all-important romance factor is quite high.

My research assistant and I ventured forth to the best local source of jasmine tea, the Golden Moon Palace Cantonese Restaurant and South Seas Cocktail Lounge. After a very fulfilling meal, we set to the task of prophecy. I downed my first cup of tea, leaving only a slight bit of liquid and loose leaves at the bottom. Then my assistant swirled the cup three times in a clockwise motion with his left hand and placed it upside-down on its saucer. After a few moments to let the liquid drain, we examined my cup. My assistant could find no clear messages in the leaf pattern, so we tried it again. This time the only messages were that I might receive a visitor or visitors sometime in the distant future and someone with the initial X (or perhaps Y or T) would soon have something to do with me, sooner or later.

I then tried to read my assistant's leaves. ❦ While working on this book, he and I were getting to know each other better, and our psychic mechanisms were getting more attuned. In his leaves I very clearly saw that things were going to go well in one part of his life but not another. He asked me for more details, so I had him drink another cup. This

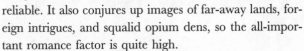

❦ It is impossible, of course, to read your own tea leaves, so all you shut-ins and agoraphobics will need to go out and find a partner for this.

time his leaves told me that he was going to go on a short journey. While I puzzled over this change in message, he announced that he had to go to the bathroom. Because the pain of a full bladder would cause terrific psychic interference, I had to let him leave the table. But what effect would this interruption have on our success thus far?

When my assistant returned, we decided that I should be the subject again. When I drank my cup this time, I left too much liquid at the bottom, and as a result, my assistant drenched the neighboring booth when he swirled the cup. After profuse apologies, I drained another cup. In the mass of leaves stuck to the bottom my assistant could see a catastrophe awaiting me in the far future. I was bursting to ask him how far, but also bursting in other, more immediate ways. This time it was my turn to "take a short journey," so I excused myself.

When I returned, my assistant was nowhere to be seen, and a busboy was cleaning our dishes off the table—including our tea cups! I tried to remain calm and explained to him that he was interrupting important research, but he pretended not to understand me. When my assistant came back from using the pay phone, he was as disappointed as I that our research had been swept away. However, he was so wired from his numerous cups of tea that he asked to be excused from further experiments for the evening. To pull rank on him and threaten to withhold his paycheck would have produced too much negative energy for effective research, so I let him go.

The waiter brought me the check in a surly manner. On the little tray were a stick of Doublemint and two fortune cookies. It occurred to me then that the evening's work might continue after all. I announced to the waiter that I wasn't finished with my meal and sent him back to the kitchen with a new order.

Tasseography Results: Inconclusive.

FORTUNE COOKIES

The friendly little after-dinner nosh known as the fortune cookie is actually part of the long history of *aleuromancy,* the art of prophetic baking. Another familiar practice in this tradition is baking a coin or ring in a cake, then giving the lucky person who finds the object a prize, like the name of a reputable dentist.

My waiter was less than pleased when I ordered 25 more fortune cookies (with more jasmine tea to wash them down), but I told him it was for scientific purposes. He might have assumed I was from the Health Department, because he brought the cookies to the table quite quickly and cheerfully. Then I got down to work.

I began by eating each cookie as I read the fortune, hoping that this ceremonial aspect would create a magic space and improve the prophecy. By the eighth or ninth one, the appeal had worn off. Because nothing I had read stated that the cookie needed to be ingested

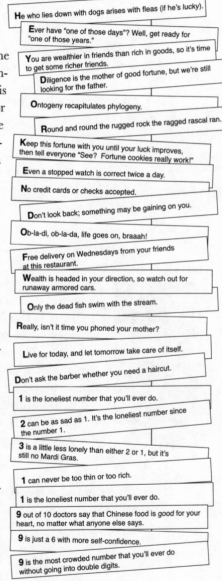

He who lies down with dogs arises with fleas (if he's lucky).

Ever have "one of those days"? Well, get ready for "one of those years."

You are wealthier in friends than rich in goods, so it's time to get some richer friends.

Diligence is the mother of good fortune, but we're still looking for the father.

Ontogeny recapitulates phylogeny.

Round and round the rugged rock the ragged rascal ran.

Keep this fortune with you until your luck improves, then tell everyone "See? Fortune cookies really work!"

Even a stopped watch is correct twice a day.

No credit cards or checks accepted.

Don't look back; something may be gaining on you.

Ob-la-di, ob-la-da, life goes on, braaah!

Free delivery on Wednesdays from your friends at this restaurant.

Wealth is headed in your direction, so watch out for runaway armored cars.

Only the dead fish swim with the stream.

Really, isn't it time you phoned your mother?

Live for today, and let tomorrow take care of itself.

Don't ask the barber whether you need a haircut.

1 is the loneliest number that you'll ever do.

2 can be as sad as 1. It's the loneliest number since the number 1.

3 is a little less lonely than either 2 or 1, but it's still no Mardi Gras.

1 can never be too thin or too rich.

1 is the loneliest number that you'll ever do.

9 out of 10 doctors say that Chinese food is good for your heart, no matter what anyone else says.

9 is just a 6 with more self-confidence.

9 is the most crowded number that you'll ever do without going into double digits.

to validate the prophecy, I continued smashing the cookies and pulling out the fortunes. Amid the debris of cookie chunks and cellophane wrappers, I spread out all my fortunes, but alas they seemed to have no pattern or relevance. Another method of prophecy had fizzled out.

For the record's sake, the previous page shows the fortunes I received in order.

Aleuromancy Results: Inconclusive.

CEPHALOMANCY

One fortune-telling method that has always intrigued me is *cephalomancy*. It involves the reading of omens that appear when a donkey's head is severed and boiled.

I would have been wise to pick another venue for it, however. When I broached the subject with my waiter (I never actually *asked* him to boil a donkey's head, I must point out), he unleashed a storm of curses so violent that the other Cantonese-speakers in the restaurant turned and started yelling at him for his unseemly abuse. I figured this was as good a time as any to make a retreat, so I ducked outside and hailed a cab.

One aspect of the future I'm pretty certain about:

He may know all, but good luck asking.

I am no longer welcome at the Golden Moon Palace Cantonese Restaurant and South Seas Cocktail Lounge.

Cephalomancy Results: Untested.

TYROMANCY

I next chose to explore the obscure method of divination known as *tyromancy,* in which the prophet peers at a vat of fermenting cheese and, as it coagulates, witnesses clues to upcoming events. A dying art, to be sure. None of the storefront fortune-tellers here in Chicago were doing much work in dairy, so I chose the most logical next step and headed for the Wisconsin border.

Seer or fermenter?

I drove north, into the heart of Dairyland USA, past the fireworks warehouses, past the outlet malls, past innumerable ex-amples of the fiberglass-animal sculptor's art. But it was difficult to find a cheesemaking operation in that great state that hadn't been mechanized and automated be-yond the recognition of Nature. Further, plant authorities and security personnel were not all that interested in learning anything about the ancient art of predictive *fro-mage.* They must have thought I was with the Board of Health too, or else was an industrial spy from a compet-ing cheesery, as they roughly sent me packing.

Desperate, I took a gamble and headed for the Wis-consin State Fair, which luckily was in full swing. I headed straight for the Agricultural Arts Building, Cheese and Curd Wing, hoping to find a wise soul who could give me some insight into divinatory fermentation. Alas, everyone I met had either never heard of tyromancy or was a conser-vative Christian who hectored me that any sort of fortune-telling, even if it involved wonderful Wisconsin cow's milk, was the work of the devil. After reaching this obviously dead end, I left with a heavy heart.

On the way out of the building, I paused to admire some of the blue ribbons in different domestic competitions—Best Pickles, Best Quilt, and so on. The Cheese Sculpting Contest especially captured my attention. The honorable mentions included a dramatic mushroom cloud carved from speckled Havarti (a political statement that one rarely sees in such competitions), a somber Stonehenge made of Muenster, and a whimsical flying saucer, complete with bug-eyed Limburger extraterrestrials. The blue-ribbon winner was a knockout: Artfully carved from vivid Colby and Pepper Jack cheeses, riding on ivory clouds of curd, was the figure of a frightening beast, with ten horns on its seven heads and a seductive-looking woman riding on its back and swilling a cup of martyr's blood (actually red-wine Cheddar). How I wish the sculptor had been there, so I could have asked him about his inspired creation.

Tyromancy Results: Incomplete.

SCARPOMANCY

This divinatory science allows a psychic to interpret another's character by examining a person's old shoes. This was admittedly a long shot, but somehow, despite my recent setbacks, my confidence in my soothsaying skills was growing. I took advantage of street-festival season here in the city and set up a folding table on the corner with a sign that read: "I WANT YOUR USED SHOES! LET ME READ YOUR CHARACTER."

If only these shoes could talk . . .

Unfortunately, this attempt went so badly I cannot bring myself to recall it. All I'll say is I am *not* a foot fetishist, and even if I were, there was no need to involve the police.

Scarpomancy Results: Negative.

CRYSTAL BALLS AND
MAGIC MIRRORS

I just knew I had to give this prophecy racket one last try. I could feel the psychic energy building up in me like an explosive cocktail of ego and impatience. And while there were many methods I had yet to try, I decided to take a stab at the classics.

Remember the movie *Snow White*? Remember her stepmother, the Evil Queen? Remember how much you envied her fashion sense and tried to copy it at school with flowing capes and tight-fitting gowns? I sure do. And I also remember her ability at forecasting the future with both a magic mirror and a crystal ball, two of the classic methods of psychic divination. Each of these is very effective and very powerful. They've been used by everyone from Merlin to the Munsters. Since my prophetic efforts had been so disappointing, I decided that perhaps my luck would change if I harnessed *both* of these forces simultaneously.

One of the most difficult maneuvers in prophecy is the 7-10 split.

Think of the surface perfection of the crystal sphere. Combine it with the reflective radiance of the mirror. What infinite possibilities would be held within a *mirrored* sphere!

Unconvinced? Then consider: Compact discs are circular and resemble mirrors on one side. They render perfect fidelity for recorded music. They can hold much more music than standard LPs. And Neil Young's recent recording *Mirror Ball* is one of the best CDs in years. See how it all comes together?

Where to find a mirror ball was my first concern. The few authentic discotheques in town catered to young, irony-drenched ravers (whose music is too loud to enable concentration) or recent immigrants from Eastern Europe and Southeast Asia (who, I'm sorry, simply smoke too damned much). On a hunch I went to a party-supply house, and there, tucked between the dunking booths and the roulette wheels, was a perfectly sized mirror ball in its own little rig, complete with tiny laser lights to create the proper *Dance Fever* atmosphere. I immediately rented the rig from the scrawny, tattooed young man behind the counter and prepared for an evening of celestial insight.

Once home, I set the rig in the middle of my living room, turned on an ambient tape recording of a waterfall with an occasional frog-croak, and switched off the lights. Settling in on a pillow on the floor, I switched on the mirror ball and opened myself to what it had to say.

Results were fast in coming. Within 20 minutes of staring at the mirror ball, I had developed a headache strong enough to jam radio signals. Within 30 minutes, my eyestrain was so bad I had to turn the thing off. I didn't bother to turn the room lights on, because wherever I looked, all I could see was a reddish-brown blur. According to my doctor, the retinal damage is probably not permanent, but for the immediate future, I'm forced to wear a pair of those huge black sunglasses favored by octogenarians.

I've never had a chance to try out my fail-safe—a chrome ball that I bought at the lawn and garden center. After the sun goes down, I sit next to the ball on its pedestal in the backyard. From what little I can see, its prophetic abilities are nil. Mainly I try to enjoy the smell of the grass and the sound of the wind in the trees. Once in a while, I can hear a frog croak.

Mirror Ball Results: Negative.

Strange Days

Pyramids, Death Rays, and Harmonicas

WHAT WOULD IT TAKE to convince you that the end of the world was near? Dogs walking on their hind legs and smoking pipes? Rain falling up and trees growing sideways? Madonna having a baby without an exclusive maternity ward broadcast on HBO? Sonny Bono being elected to the U.S. Congress?

Admit it, that last picture is almost too ridiculous to imagine, yet it *did* happen. *Twice!* These are strange days we live in, whatever yardstick you use.

Evidence that the end times have arrived is all around us. Consider the state of today's world, to start off. Never in all of history has there been such upheaval,

violence, famine, and despair (at least, if you don't bother to read your history books very closely). Every day satellites beam television signals into our homes showing chaos, destruction, vengeance, and fearful cynicism—and when you've had enough of *ESPN SportsCenter,* you can turn to ESPN2 for the Se-

Frightening and inconceivable portents.

niors Luge Tour. These disturbing images cannot be wished away or ignored, even if you use the mute button on the remote.

While we've had a good laugh at the expense of doomsday prophets (in fact, if you want to read the previous sections again, we'll wait), were they truly wrong in their estimates of destruction? So what if they got their dates a little confused? Did *you* ever forget a birthday, Mr. Wisenheimer and Ms. Smarty-Pants? Then stop throwing stones.

All the supposed snafus of the prophets make much more sense if we consider them as a part of history, important pieces of a continuum of esoteric intelligence that has existed on earth far longer than previously imagined. This cross-disciplinary acumen, coming from such diverse fields as archaeology, astronomy, and geo-psychology, is only now being comprehended.

This exciting knowledge is often denigrated as being "fringe" science, but just because its proponents either have no scientific credentials or don't bother to seek the agreement of other experts in the field doesn't mean it lacks validity. Believe me, when everything comes crashing down, scientific credentials will make a mighty flimsy umbrella.

This chapter will examine many strange phenomena that have enormous importance for the future of our planet. We will look deep into the past and project far into the future. You might want to pack a light lunch and a change of underwear. And leave your skepticism behind.

ATLANTIS

CRYSTALS AND CRUSTACEANS

PLATO WAS THE FIRST Western commentator to mention the lost continent of Atlantis, more than 2,300 years ago. As he told his students (after he'd taken over the class when his Ph.D. advisor Socrates was charged with corrupting the morals of Athenian youth, thus putting a serious crimp in Plato's tenure track),

> THE ISLAND WAS LARGER THAN LIBYA
> AND ASIA PUT TOGETHER, AND WAS THE
> WAY TO OTHER ISLANDS, AND FROM
> THE ISLANDS YOU MIGHT PASS
> THROUGH THE WHOLE OF THE OPPOSITE
> CONTINENT WHICH SURROUNDED THE
> TRUE OCEAN. . . . NOW, IN THE ISLAND
> OF ATLANTIS THERE WAS A GREAT AND
> WONDERFUL EMPIRE. . . .

Plato was the smartest man in the entire world, correct? So it would be nearly impossible to fool him into accepting hearsay and folklore as historical truth, wouldn't you agree? Ergo, Atlantis must have existed just as he said.❡

While the idea of lost continents and forgotten civilizations has intrigued humankind throughout history, the popularity of Atlantis has grown phenomenally in the past 100 years. It has been conservatively estimated that 25,000 books have been written about Atlantis around the world. While some readers may assume the story is only useful as an inspiration for comic books and bad television shows, the existence of Atlantis, if true, holds great importance for us end-of-the-world rubberneckers: It would demonstrate that humanity has been destroyed on a large scale more than once. It might even give us the keys to our survival.

According to Plato, Edgar Cayce, and others, Atlantis flourished from 75,000 to 12,000 years ago, a large land mass that stretched from the Caribbean to the Straits of Gibraltar. The Atlanteans' incredibly advanced civilization ran on the power of gigantic quartz crystals, set in observatory-like domes. According to Cayce, these "fire stones" were marvelously efficient, gathering solar, lunar, stellar, atmospheric, and earth energies, as well as undefined elemental forces.❡❡ These energies were used to power aircraft, submarines, broadcasting systems, computers, and an early version of the Nintendo 64 home video game. Atlantean technology also developed a death ray, something no advanced civilization can do without. Sure, America may have put a man on the moon, but we don't have anything nearly as cool as a death ray. Damned congressional penny-pinchers! Write

❡For those of you enrolled in community college, I just demonstrated a *syllogism*, a philosophic device popular among ancient Greek thinkers and logicians. By using it to prove the existence of Atlantis, I was making a bit of a self-referential joke.

❡❡Lunar, stellar, atmospheric, and earth energies remain undefined at the present time as well.

your representative today and demand increased funding for death-ray research!

Everything was going—*ahem*—swimmingly in Atlantis until someone decided to use the power of crystals for evil instead of good (yet another instance of life imitating a James Bond movie). According to Cayce, "The downfall of Atlantis was caused through the gross misuse and abuse of all the sacred knowledge and energies by certain evil priests, who only sought eternal power and corruption." In other words, just like Darth Vader succumbing to the dark side of the Force, it's the same old same old.

The most popular place that never was (maybe).

These corrupt priests, known as the Sons of Belial, were a greedy and hedonistic bunch, and used their sacred knowledge, hypnotic skills, and crystal powers for materialistic ends and the seduction of young, crystal-powered priestesses. By cranking up the fire stones full blast, they upset the balance of nature and brought about the destruction of their island-continent. This happened not once but *three* different times—in 50,000 B.C.E., 28,000 B.C.E. and finally 10,000 B.C.E. (the Atlantean affinity for mass destruction in neat, even millennial years offers much food for thought as the zeroes line up for the year 2000).

The Sons of Belial had as their counterparts the good Atlanteans, followers of the "Law of One." They sought to uphold the purer spiritual traditions that made Atlantis great. But they couldn't compete with those hypnotic, fun-loving SOBs. Luckily, the earthquakes, floods, and volcanic eruptions that destroyed Atlantis occurred at multicentury intervals, which gave the good guys, our heroes, the followers of the Law of One (yay!), time to prepare. The Law-of-Oners were able to skedaddle via airship and boat to Egypt, Peru, Mexico, and other places, where they instructed the benighted natives in advanced Atlantean knowledge and showed them how to build pyramids.

Before the complete destruction of Atlantis, the followers of the Law of One decided to hide or destroy the blueprints for their crystal technologies to keep them from falling into the wrong hands. Some priests and priestesses "programmed" quartz crystals with vital information on the Atlantean lifestyle, history, and scientific achievements. According to certain psychics, many of these "record-keeper" crystals are now returning to our physical consciousness, making themselves known to us and disrupting conventional methods in library science. The information contained within the crystals is slowly being absorbed into our bodies and minds. Only when the time is right will we know all.

To coincide with this, the spirits of many Atlanteans are being reincarnated in our present lifetime, bringing with them the ancient wisdom of a wrecked continent. Most of these are coming back in America, particularly (and not surprisingly) in California. They exist among us, undercover rather than underwater, and will help us all enter a new age when a sufficient number of them arrive. So, if anyone you meet exudes a certain knowledgeability about quartz crystals as well as a slightly fishy odor, pay close attention to what they have

The best offense is a good death ray.

to say. They may be the heralds of a glorious era for humanity, and not just slightly smelly creeps. ❛

Danger still lurks ahead, however. Along with the good Atlanteans, many wicked Atlanteans are also being reincarnated. These nasties are still intent on eternal power and corruption (boo!). You can tell who they are because they are actively working to discredit and hinder the progress of crystal healers, who still uphold the Law of One (yay!). These reborn Belials would have you believe that a quartz crystal is just a shiny rock, but don't you believe them, or it will spell doom for us all. The fate of the entire world is in your hands, Mr. Bond!

If the story of Atlantis turns out to be true, it would

❛If it is true that the spirits of many Atlanteans are now being reincarnated, then a ready-made audience was in place for *Waterworld*. So why was the movie such a bomb? I have no answer, but my gut instinct tells me that moviegoers, whatever their background, are not yet ready for a big-screen hero with prune hands.

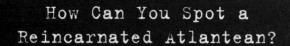

How Can You Spot a Reincarnated Atlantean?

Check their feet.

Regular person   Reincarnated Atlantean

Applications of Atlantean Crystal Technology

shatter our notions of the longevity of human civilization. It would also give credence to the notion that the world has ended before, with strong parallels to the Great Flood described in the Bible and in most cultures around the world. Some psychic researchers, striving to prove that Edgar Cayce was right, assert that a portion of Atlantis is resurfacing now off the coast of Bimini. Is it a coincidence that these supposed Atlantean ruins are so close to the mysterious area known as the Bermuda Triangle? Or that former presidential candidate Gary Hart was caught philandering off the coast of Bimini on the good ship *Monkey Business*? Well, yes, actually it is a coincidence, but that shouldn't detract from the credibility of our argument thus far.

THE GREAT PYRAMID OF CHEOPS

INCHES FROM DOOM

When studying the dimensions of the pyramids, don't drop your pencil or it'll roll halfway to Cairo.

ANCIENT MYSTERIES BROOD silently in the Land of the Pharaohs. Across the desert sands, the Sphinx stares voicelessly, noselessly. The camel chews his cud breathlessly, while its handler watches wordlessly, and his child shouts shamelessly, "Need a guide? Need a guide? Camel ride, ten bucks American! Come on! Come on!" And behind all, looming heedlessly, is the Great Pyramid of Cheops.

The oldest, largest, and last surviving of the Seven Wonders of the Ancient World, the Great Pyramid is a marvel of engineering. Its multi-ton bricks were mined many miles away from the site at Gizeh, and today fit together as snugly as multi-ton bricks. According to some commentators (but not, we should note, the American Institute of Architects), this superior level of construction would be impossible to achieve with today's building techniques, union or non-union. Therefore, we must presume the pyramid was built by survivors of Atlantis. Or maybe aliens. But not those lazy, squabbling, good-for-nothing Egyptians. ❧

Another fascinating aspect of the Great Pyramid is the arcane measurements contained within its dimensions. Ever since it was rediscovered by the West in Napoleon's time, scientists, mathematicians, landscape architects, and interior designers (including Charles Taze Russell, founder of the Jehovah's Witnesses) have worked ceaselessly with pencil and tape measure to discover the true importance of the pyramid and the advanced knowledge of its builders. In fact, the structure is a treasure trove of technical and earth-science data.

For example, when the perimeter of the pyramid's base is divided by twice its height, the result is 3.1416, or pi. Of course, it would be nearly impossible to smuggle a pyramid into a geometry exam, but the importance of this remains undisputed. Also, when you multiply the weight of the Great Pyramid by one trillion, you get the approximate weight of the earth. When you multiply the base perimeter by the weight and divide by 0.016, you get a very, very large number indeed. And the volume of the structure is exactly equal to the volume of one *Great Pyramid of Cheops!* Certainly, these are more than mere coincidences.

❧ One of the most fascinating questions surrounding the pyramid is how its huge stones traveled from the quarry to the building site several miles away. The Egyptians could have used slave labor to pull them on rollers (unlike the Maya, the Egyptians had the wheel), but that answer is so literal and mundane as to be unsatisfying. So for many New Agers, the answer is levitation. Through songs and mysterious chanting, the stones moved through the air under their own power, like the stelae of Stonehenge. If this is true, we can deduce that the pyramid was built with scab labor, since union rules wouldn't have allowed such labor-saving vocalizations.

Even more important than its use as a paperweight is the Great Pyramid's design as a historical diorama, a 3-D prophetic blueprint, a march of the millennial mile in miniature. In other words, we can use the pyramid as more than just the backdrop for Grateful Dead concerts; we can actually use it for (as if you couldn't guess by now) predicting the end of the world.

The pyramid contains numerous passageways that lead in different directions, most notably to the main burial chamber. It has been conjectured that these passageways are actually an elaborate time line for the history and fate of the earth. Numbers are not carved into the masonry, however, nor does the pyramid recite any historical details. Rather, we must interpret the turns in

Is Our Planet AC or DC?

According to psychic researcher Moira Timms, the Great Pyramid "is the primary sacred site of the world, on the master node of the planetary grid." Come again? The planetary grid is an invisible network of energy paths that serve as meridians for all sorts of energies in the earth. At their geographic intersections, these paths form power nodes. All ancient sacred sites, says Timms, are located on power nodes.

For those of you who, like me, are intimidated by something as simple as a dashboard fuse box, this notion of a worldwide energy grid may be daunting. Don't be frightened—the earth energies are available to everyone, handy with a tool or not, to use in their spiritual growth. Just remember to wear rubber-soled shoes.

the corridors, the colors in the stones, and other details to match historical events.

The key to unlocking the mysteries of the passage-ways lies just inside the entrance, next to a souvenir stand and behind a map rack. In the stone wall are scored two parallel vertical lines—what enthusiasts on the subject have dubbed the pyramid-inch. Using this measurement, and equating a pyramid-inch to one stan-dard (i.e., nonpyramidal) year, it is possible to discern the entire history of mankind within the ancient corridors.

Our tour starts at the entrance of the pyramid, which equates to the year 4004 B.C.E., the classic, bibli-cally based date for the creation of the world as calcu-lated by Bishop James Ussher. From there you walk down a steep slope (symbolizing the fall of mankind after Adam and Eve), descending many years and pyramid-inches until you hit 1615 B.C.E., the date the Israelites were freed from Egyptian slavery and given the Ten Commandments. You then walk up 1648 years—excuse me, inches—excuse me, *pyramid*-inches—to arrive at the death of Jesus in 33 C.E. and the establishment of a new covenant between Yahweh and all people, Jews and Gentiles alike.

At this point, a horizontal hallway branches off as the ascending passage continues. A spiritually symbolic detour or a simple access tunnel for the royal caterers? Make of it what you will. The ascending passage then takes us to the Grand Gallery, whose spacious dimen-sions are symbolic of the expansion of consciousness brought on by the Christian era. Watch where you're go-ing or you'll conk your head on 1844, a date, according to psychic Moira Timms, "when the seed was germi-nated for collective humanity to awaken to a global awareness of itself as a single consciousness." Timms is referring to the founding of the Baha'i faith in Persia.

This year also witnessed the patenting of vulcanized rubber. Coincidence? Hardly.

The Grand Gallery ends at 1914, the beginning of the First World War. From this point on, the pyramid-inch stands for a month rather than a year, for unclear reasons (other than it makes the whole megillah work). We will also begin to crawl on our hands and knees a while, as we enter the Antechamber to the King's Chamber. Scamper through here and you'll smack your forehead on the end of the world, represented by a stone called the Granite Leaf, on September 17, 2001.

Why this date? The calculations are somewhat arcane, and many other dates have been posited with varying degrees of plausibility. But you will notice that from the pyramid entrance (4004 B.C.E.) to the Granite Leaf (2001 C.E.) is roughly 6,000 years—the exact age and expiration date of the earth, if you take the Bible literally. How nice that Christian fundamentalists and New Age pyramidologists can find something in common here!

Pyramids are not exclusive to Egypt, of course. They can also be found in the jungles of Central and South America and the Middle East's Fertile Crescent. Many hypotheses have sought to explain this: that a pyramid is the most stable structure you can build, and thus best survives the passage of time; that ancient societies venerated the concept of the "holy hill" and sought closer contact with their gods by building toward the sky; that there weren't enough scaffolds to go around; and so on. But I think the most comprehensive yet elegant solution is this: The pyramids were an early form of motor hotel, not unlike a Howard Johnson's or Holiday Inn, and their distinctive shape was a welcome sight to the weary traveler. The pyramids and ziggurats may indeed have been built by space aliens or survivors of Atlantis, but the ana-

Yankees of the Damned

Few public buildings in modern America combine the religious, political, and sociological importance of the pyramids, but Yankee Stadium comes pretty close. The House That Ruth Built is full of legends and myths, and there is no more important place to watch a baseball game (if I can use "important" and "baseball game" in the same sentence these days). So inquiring minds like ours are compelled to ask, "What secrets are locked within the physical dimensions of this magnificent structure?"

For our benchmark measurement, absent a pyramid-inch, the only logical choice is the length of a regular Kahn's hot dog, as sold throughout the stadium and in the stands. Applying the "dog-inch" to the dimensions of the stadium, we find:

> Perimeter at exterior ground level = 185,769 dog-inches, or roughly the speed of light

> Height above main gate (minus flagpoles) = 12,520 dog-inches, or roughly the diameter of the earth

Furthermore:

> Approximate distance to sun/Speed of light = 714, or Babe Ruth's career home run tally

Ample evidence by any standard.

If we bring our hot dog inside and apply it to the
playing field, more mysteries unfold. We take the
backstop as our beginning, and call it the year 1 C.E.
Heading toward center field, we find:

Home plate = 33 C.E., Christ's crucifixion year

Apex of pitcher's mound = 1000 C.E., a nice round
number and the date of the first millennium[*]

Second base = 1215 C.E., the year of the signing of
the Magna Carta[**]

Center field storm drain = 1776, the year of the
signing of the Declaration of Independence[***]

Warning track = 1945, the end of World War II and the
dropping of the atomic bomb

Outfield fence = 1961, the year Roger Maris hit 61
home runs, breaking Ruth's single-season record

Babe Ruth Monument = 1973, the introduction of the
designated hitter rule (and, some would argue, the
first nail in baseball's coffin)[****]

Terminal wall = 2000 C.E.

Coincidence?

[*] If we begin to lay the hot dog sideways.
[**] We took a hefty bite at the pitcher's mound, the dog looked so good.
[***] At this point we are using a foot-long, as the vendor was
completely out of regular dogs.
[****] By now, we have completely consumed the hot dog, just as the
Babe would have done. From here to the wall, we are using the
length of a mustard packet.

lyst who ponder these ideas have omitted an important person from their formulas: the franchisee.

This ancient concept in hospitality lives on today in one of the brightest new stars on the Las Vegas strip, the Luxor Hotel. An immense glass pyramid with elevators that climb up the sloping sides (and have thus been dubbed "inclinators"), the Luxor features its own Sphinx and copy of Cleopatra's Needle, indoor barge ride, theme restaurants (one of which is portentously named "Millennium"), and, of course, casino. Some people also claim that, during a stay at the Luxor, your razors always stay sharp.

If the Atlanteans were so advanced, why weren't any attractions like this included in the Great Pyramid of Cheops? Imperial Egypt might have forestalled its collapse if its people had worked to attract more convention business.

Perhaps the most striking element of the Luxor Hotel is the spotlight that beams out of its apex straight up into the desert sky. According to the hotel's management, it is the largest laser beam in the world and can be seen from ten miles up in space! A beacon for the weary space traveler, perhaps? If this is indeed a celestial "Vacancy" sign, and off-world visitors stop in, what must be their first impression of our species and our concepts of entertainment, art, commerce, and feminine beauty (when all the women in Vegas are either five foot two and dressed in polyester, or six foot six and filled with silicone)? Then again, everybody likes Siegfried and Roy, no matter what the color of their skin or the capacity of their brain pans. And if aliens do come, their tourist dollars are as good as anyone's.

UFOS

FETISHISTS FROM THE FUTURE?

IT SEEMS EVERYWHERE you look these days, the paranormal is out there. Movies, books, television shows, celebrity murder trials—the stories are weird, unnerving, and completely unpredictable. Much of the popularity of this unusual business is a result of the impending end of the century and our anxiety about the future we face. Just like the 1950s, the last heyday of science fiction movies, the times we live in are tense and uncertain.

The truth is out there—but is it just cruisin'?

It is a fact that, for the past two or three hundred years, sightings of unidentified flying objects have increased toward the end of each century. This has been true in spades as we approach the end of the 20th. Are the alien visitors coming for a specific purpose, or just to browse the "End-of-the-Century" sales? Perhaps the UFO pilots are merely looking for a good New Year's party, or their summer vacations only come every 100 years. Apart from the opportunity for a few abductions and a cattle mutilation here and there, why are more and more aliens including earth in their vacation plans? There are many hypotheses.

One school of thought stresses that the extraterrestrials are generous and enlightened teachers—perhaps even a version of ourselves, several centuries in the future—who are trying to assist us in our own evolution. They have been visiting our planet for eons and have helped us along at different stages of civilization's development. They were the ones who built the pyramids, of course, as well as Stonehenge and the heads on Easter Island (perhaps an arts-and-crafts project for alien tykes that got out of hand?). Obviously humans aren't smart enough to have designed and built these mysterious energy mechanisms, or else why would the aliens need to keep coming back to show us how they work?

Many people believe that aliens will be able to lead us into a more enlightened era. Numerous psychic channelers have been in contact with intergalactic intelligences, whom they refer to as "ascended masters,"❡ "space brothers," or "white brethren" (referring to the light their bodies transmit, not to their affinity for conquest and exploitation). These teachers will show us how to awaken the power of the human spirit so that we can enter into a period of paradise on earth. By focusing on messages of peace, love, and understanding, we can position ourselves for the beginning of a New Age—a quantum leap in our evolution on both a physical and spiritual level. It's time to discard the old stereotypes; aliens who destroy cities and gobble human brains are the stuff of imagination.

Our space brothers (and sisters, no doubt, if we knew where to look to check) will teach us many important lessons. Chief among them, according to top psychics, will be how to rise to higher levels of "vibration." The rest of the universe is already vibrating at this higher level, and we desperately need to catch up.❡❡ Our new

As a species, are we destined to evolve into cheap lounge acts?

❡ Not to be confused with Elizabeth Clare Prophet's "Ascended Masters" or with the many fine products of the StairMaster Corporation.

❡❡ A good way to explore the potential of your own vibratory rate is to purchase a Magic Fingers or electric La-Z-Boy recliner for your home. For more advanced study in liberating yourself, many mail-order catalogs, such as Good Vibrations, offer discreet, convenient delivery of personal "vibration aids" right to your door.

Crop Circles:
Sarcasm from the Stars?

Recent years have seen an increase in crop circle activity in Europe, North America, and parts of Asia. The simple yet intriguing shapes that previously were pressed into wheat fields have given way to more elaborate designs, suggesting everything from fractal patterns to double helixes. What goes unreported, however, are the many imprints that appear to be nothing more than taunting distractions or smart-alecky "crop graffiti." Judge for yourself the maturity level of so-called "advanced beings" from the designs they've left:

"shake rate," for lack of a better term, will allow us to enter previously unknown dimensions and develop new senses beyond sight and smell. We will be able to perceive the energy auras that surround all living things and not just portraits of Chairman Mao and "Precious Moments" figurines. In time, we will be able to communicate telepathically, extend our healthy lives, and evolve into beings of pure psychic energy.

What will happen if we fail to heed this call for vibratory self-improvement? Major earth changes and terrible catastrophes, of course. These disasters will not destroy humankind, but will cleanse the planet of those who reject the teachings of this new era. Those who are receptive to the help offered by our space pals will be whisked away safely into their spaceships, while the rest of the rabble die in floods, earthquakes, volcanic eruptions, and the like (another similarity between New Agers and fundamentalists). Then the enlightened ones will return and repopulate the earth with smarter, saner, more evolved humans with improved vibratory patterns (or "vibes," as the hippie types used to say).

That's one viewpoint. Another school of thought contends that these ETs are evil and intent on ruling the world. Some personal accounts of alien abduction—with deceptions, threats, medical experiments, anal probes, and the like—would seem to bolster this less optimistic theory. Here's an advanced race of beings who possess vast knowledge of physics, biology, and galactic travel, and they still find time for a quick trip to earth to do raunchy things to innocent bystanders? Sounds like an interstellar fraternity road trip to me.

Abductees have testified that aliens are able to change their shape and appearance, become invisible, paralyze their victims, and perform other nasty tricks. These bug-eyed kidnappers claim that the earth will soon form one government and that through improved vibratory skills humans will be able to become like gods. These offers to lead humans into an earthly paradise technically make the aliens false messiahs. For these and other reasons, some Christians have deduced that aliens are actually a race of demons, headed by Lucifer himself, who have camped out on other planets since their expulsion from heaven. Soon the space demons plan to attack earth and make it their own, in line with the accounts of Armageddon in the Book of Revelation. Who says Christian fundamentalists need to be dragged kicking and screaming into the 20th century? They're already living in the 21st—and maybe beyond.

Telepathy: What's It to Ya?

Many psychics and New Age devotees feel that we will evolve into beings able to communicate merely by thought waves. But would telepathy really be a boon to humanity? Below is a partial list of activities that would be endangered, if not completely eliminated, by widespread telepathy:

POKER. Bluffing with two pair would hardly hold the thrill it does now.

POLITICS. Without the ability to deceive, what politician could ever get elected?

FASHION. No one would have to wait for the answer to "How does this make me look?"

SEX. Never again could anything be faked, forced, fudged, or forgotten.

MARRIAGE. See above.

The deceptive nature of these devils is quite obvious if you look at the propaganda they've been spreading in recent times. Aliens are either cute and whimsical (*E.T., Mork and Mindy, My Favorite Martian*), no match for human cunning and bravery (*Independence Day, Alien*), or bizarre but harmless (*3rd Rock from the Sun*, Quisp cereal). Good Christians can tell, however, that a pair of antennae on the back of the head are just a disguise for a pair of horns in front.

A third school of thought is that these extraterrestrials are neither deliverers nor devils but merely a band of kinky pranksters. Abductees' stories of group sex, weird tattoos, and rectal dowsing rods, combined with the evidence of crop circles increasing around the world, suggest images of rebellious teens who have swiped the keys to Dad's Mercury Mark CCLXXIV and gone joyriding through the sleazier parts of the galaxy.

You say you need evidence for this theory? Consider the aliens' sense of direction, to start. With all the achievements of mankind for them to observe and explore, and all the natural marvels of earth to ponder, where do most UFO sightings occur? The marshlands of Michigan and the Ozark Mountains. From this one could hypothesize that aliens are avid bass fishermen, or prefer locales with cheap beer and easy-to-obtain fireworks.❡

And the supposed crash in Roswell, New Mexico? Perhaps someone was "overserved" while gambling in Vegas and wrapped his flying machine around a lamppost. With all the panic that these space punks create, some sort of curfew might be the answer.

This is perhaps the most unsettling and unsavory possibility, one that our pride makes very hard to stom-

❡I assume that, if they wanted to, the music fans of an advanced society would be able to listen to the shows of Branson, Missouri, by remote somehow. Or, more likely, blast it from the face of the earth, which brings us back to the "benevolent alien" theory.

ach: Aliens don't care enough to either guide us into a new age *or* invade and dominate our planet. They're just here to use us. To them, we're just a cheap date, easy to impress and a cinch to dump. I don't want to think about it. The whole idea just makes me feel so . . . dirty.

HARMONIC CONVERGENCE AND THE MAYA FACTOR

In 1987, A MYSTIC and "planetary whole systems anthropologist" named José Argüelles made headlines around the world (though admittedly smaller than the Iran-Contra investigation or the tenth anniversary of Elvis's death) with news of a once-in-a-lifetime chance for the earth to attach cables to its collective consciousness and jumpstart it to the next evolutionary level. Meditations on peace and unity, if prayed by a certain critical mass of humanity, would allow us to purge the planet of war, hunger, and other misfortunes.

What would make this effort more powerful than your average prayer-a-thon? The gravitational force of most of the planets in our solar system. On August 16–17, 1987, a lion's share of the planets would be aligned within a tight arc emanating from the sun. In this type of arrangement, a great deal of cosmic energy would be shoveled into a small space and would bathe our whole planet in positive vibrations, if the gravitational forces didn't destroy it with earthquakes and volcanoes first.

Argüelles coined the term "Harmonic Convergence" for this event, but the concept has been around for centuries. It's usually called a planetary alignment, and its power has been an obsession for astrologers and prophets. Numerous times they've predicted that a planetary alignment would destroy the world (see sidebar for a partial list), but in our modern age, we're too sophisticated to see this event as nothing but fire and brimstone. It's actually a special opportunity for personal and planetary growth. As we might paraphrase, "When Life hands you a Harmonic Convergence, get out your harmonica and converge."

So during those August days in 1987, people gath-

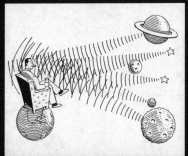

The parallels between acoustic science and "vibrational space energy" science are helpful in understanding many of these New Age concepts. This does not mean, however, that you need "some really kick-ass speakers" to become enlightened.

Hey, Got Room for One More?

Full moons are blamed for inciting chaos on earth, so it
stands to reason that the gravitational power of whole planets would cause a big ruckus. Many times in the past our fellow planetary wanderers have crowded into our neighborhood,
and the predicted results have been dire.

September 1186

In 1179, John of Toledo foretold catastrophe when all the
known planets united under the sign of Libra. Many thousands
across the Mediterranean believed him, including the Byzantine emperor, who had his palace windows boarded over for
safety. After nothing happened, John announced that he was
actually making a symbolic prediction of the European invasion of the Huns, and so had been correct all along. (The
poor Huns—they get blamed for everything.)

December 17, 1919

In a small Italian-language newspaper in San Francisco, seis-
mologist and weatherman Albert Porta predicted that a conjunc-
tion of six planets on this date would result in a magnetic
current, which would pierce the sun and ignite explosions of
flaming gas that would swallow the earth. As the day ap-
proached, reports of suicide and hysteria were rampant. After
nothing happened, Porta went back to predicting the weather.
I'd like to see Willard Scott command such attention!

February 2, 1962

This date saw eight planets cram themselves into the House of
Capricorn, the first such event in 400 years. Astrologers in
India said this would begin the end of the world, which in-
flamed millions of people on the subcontinent. In one
marathon prayer meeting to Chandi Path, the goddess of power,
worried worshippers burned 1.5 tons of pure butter, along
with thousands of marigolds. The prime minister of Burma released three bullocks, three pigs, nine goats, 60 hens, 60
ducks, 120 doves, and 218 crabs, in hopes of appeasing the
evil forces of destruction. Apparently he was successful.

ered in small groups to accomplish what one writer described as "the evolutionary imperative of aligning human consciousness with the new energies emanating from the galactic core." Some traveled to power centers of the planetary grid, like Peru's Macchu Pichu, Japan's Mount Fuji, England's Stonehenge, and the Grand Canyon, and meditated from sunup to sundown. Others nipped out to the backyard for a quick one after coffee. And they prayed and prayed that we could push ourselves over the brink—in a *good* way, of course.

By all accounts, this convergence was a big success. You might not have noticed much change—still fighting with your family, still want a better job, still need to exercise more, etc.—but these kinds of things are hard to measure. Planet-wide shifts in consciousness, after all, can be very, very subtle.

But was the Harmonic Convergence just the beginning—or the beginning of the end? According to Argüelles, this planetary arrangement was a key event in the ancient Mayan calendar, a complex series of cycles within cycles crafted by an ancient race obsessed with the measurement of time. The convergence year of 1987, in the very convoluted Mayan cosmic system, marked the coming of the end of the *baktun* (400-year cycle) of the Transformation of Matter, the collapse of civilization, and the purification and regeneration of the world. We're also at the end of a 26,000-year cycle of regular old *Homo sapiens* inhabiting the planet. The Mayan 5,125-year calendar cycle, which began in 3113 B.C.E., is coming around to its beginning on the winter solstice, December 21, 2012 C.E. In other words, in 2012, each and every cycle in the Mayans' sinewy, complicated method of measuring time is over. Finito. Kaput. Please be careful driving home, and don't forget to tip your waitress.

What follows is up for debate. According to Argüelles,

we will enter an era of information science, crystal-solar technology, and galactic synchronization, but only if we become receptive to and align ourselves spiritually with the rest of the cosmos. If we blow this chance, we'll find ourselves in a galactic backwater, still reliant on using our mouths to communicate and our bodies to get around. Too bad for us if we become the Alabama of the universe.

Others say that the superhuman wheat will be separated from the human chaff. Those people on earth who are attuned to the cosmic forces will rule this and other worlds, while those who aren't will wallow in their backwardness like Neanderthals. The enlightened will conduct the energies of the universe through their consciousness, while the rest of us will be eating potato chips and sitting in our underwear, watching a pay-per-view broadcast of *America's Funniest Home Videos: The Movie*. Once again, we hold our fate in our hands. And where are yours right this minute?

Of course, mystery still surrounds the ancient Maya themselves. Who were they, and where did they go? Our incomplete record of them allows all sorts of notions to be projected onto this early society, especially by researchers who like to show off their math skills. Surely the image of maniacally number-crunching astronomers is someone's idea of a perfect civilization.❧ Others are withholding judgment. Can you imagine how much wall space would be taken up by a calendar with a 63,312,328-year cycle? Their Hallmark stores must have been enormous.

Archaeologists tell us that the classical Mayan civi-

❧ Considering the recent popularity of Native American spirituality among diverse ethnic groups (well, really only among middle-class Anglos), why has there been no similar interest in Mayan or Aztec religious practices? While the human sacrifices are an obvious stumbling block, it might have more to do with the clumsy hieroglyphic alphabet. And the big headdresses really don't flatter anybody, either.

lization collapsed around 843 C.E., with no obvious explanation. Could it be that, when they saw the end of global civilization that their calendars forecast, they simply gave up? Was what they saw so terrible? Were they so busy with calculations that no one remembered to plant corn? Were there "calendar wars" with other tribes in the Yucatán? We can only speculate.

Flashy religious headdress or alien space helmet? Only a showgirl knows for sure.

To Argüelles, the Mayans actually were (and still are) beings from another galaxy who transmit themselves from one star system to another encoded in strands of DNA. They planted themselves here on earth many years ago while the planet passed through a "galactic beam," and, in addition, a "great moment of transformation awaits us at beam's end in 2012." This is hard to argue with, especially if you take the word "beam" to mean a large wooden support structure that you never notice until it smacks you in the head.

For all the skills the Maya displayed at time measurement and synchronization, one must still face the unkind question: Would you buy a wristwatch from them?

CELESTINE PROPHECY

CELESTIAL PROFUNDITY OR CELLULAR PROFANITY?

IS IT MERE COINCIDENCE that so many ancient measurements of time are winding down within the next 15 years? Well, by now an astute reader would know that nothing is a coincidence if it happens to bolster the conclusions we already seek. This is how we professionals discover the messages hidden in seemingly disparate objects or events.

If the universe consists if pure energy, why are my utility bills so high?

The idea of coincidence is a central element to *The Celestine Prophecy,* beyond question the best-selling New Age book ever. And it's surely no coincidence that the book has spawned a sequel (one so far, anyway), a newsletter, seminars, study guides, posters, calendars, a CD of "official" music (with snappy titles such as "The Quest for Unity" and "Jensen—The Energy Thief"), and other paraphernalia. (Is it coincidence that the book is published by a globe-spanning telecommunications octopus like Time Warner? Or is that what they call "marketing synergy"?)

The book's plot, such as it is, concerns a dissatisfied American who discovers an ancient manuscript in Peru containing such vital truths that both the Peruvian government and the Catholic church want to suppress and destroy it. The story is merely a vehicle for author James

Redfield's spiritual insights, one of which is that coincidences are actually events provided by our mysterious but benevolent universe to guide us toward our destiny. This destiny is our evolution as spiritual beings, helped along by the realization that the universe consists of pure energy that responds to our intentions. And as soon as we stop trying to suck the energy out of each other and give our own energy more freely, we will be happier, more fulfilled, and better rested (and we'll learn to appreciate nature better, too). As we begin to fulfill our destiny by evolving spiritually, we will actually begin to increase our vibrational frequency. Finally, someone tells us how to do this.

The best part? As we all continue to increase our vibrations to a lighter and more spiritual frequency, whole groups of us will learn to become invisible! (Ironically, these people will be so evolved that they won't even think of using their special power to rob banks, pull practical jokes, or spy on people in locker rooms, like any normal person would.) Turning invisible will mean we have finally crossed the barrier between this life and the other world, from which we came and where we go after death. This is the purpose of human existence and history: to reach a heaven on earth by vibrating. So sects like the Shakers and the Whirling Dervishes have it all wrong. Shaking and spinning won't help you get to heaven. Only vibrating will.

Or something like that. Or not.

This remarkable book raises quite a few important questions:

Would you call it a coincidence that the precious manuscript discovered in Peru by the book's hero is written in ancient Aramaic, a Middle Eastern language?
No; that's probably just pretentious and unbelievable narrative clutter.

Is there a way to boost someone's vibrational frequency through the use of small personal appliances?
Probably not, but it's worth a try.

Is it a coincidence that this book has been on the New York Times *best-seller list for more than 150 weeks?*
No; it's just a sign of our chaotic times.

Is it a coincidence that "prophet" and "profit" sound the same but are spelled differently?
No; they are what language experts call *homonyms*.

Would you call it a coincidence that the author didn't exhaust all the ancient insights in his first book, but rather kept one in reserve for his sequel, The Tenth Insight?
No; there's another word for it, but it escapes me now.

These Won't Get You Vibrating

The Celestine Prophecy, like any successful book, has spawned a host of imitators, jumping on the ancient Peruvian-Aramaic vibrating-manuscript bandwagon. These are pale imitations of the insights found in the original, so caveat emptor.

The Cellophane Prophecy. As our souls grow in wisdom and power, they become rainbow-hued, lighter, and more transparent, yet at the same time brittle and highly flammable.

The Philistine Prophecy. As we evolve as a species, we complain more about why NEA artists don't take a clue from Phantom and give their audiences something they would enjoy seeing, instead of that crazy junk they call art.

The Cellulite Prophecy. Our souls can get rid of unsightly bulges and saddlebags through special exercises and liposuction.

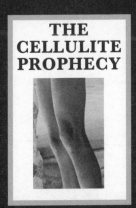

THE CELLULITE PROPHECY

The Celestite Prophecy. Humanity is being drawn to its true destiny as small lumps of powdery white mineral consisting of strontium sulfate.

The Sizzlean Prophecy. Our souls contain 66 percent less fat and sodium than ordinary meat-based souls.

My Search for Enlight- enment

All Vibed Up and Nowhere to Go

Y NOW I WAS GETTING supremely frustrated. The more I learned, the less I seemed to know. There was something happening here—big, important, literally earth-shattering—but it was moving much faster than I could keep up with. According to all I was uncovering, the entire world is on the threshold of a new age, when all humanity will make the transition from superstitious, money-grubbing, exploitative maniacs to enlightened, benevolent super-beings of wholly psychic energy. And me—I can't even get my socks off (figuratively speaking).

Had I lived in Atlantis during its crystal-powered heyday? I don't know. Had I been abducted by a UFO, probed and sampled, then brain-wiped and dumped back in the middle of a cow pasture, "Wham-Bam, Thanks, Earth Man"? I don't know! Did I have my own way of seeing the world that I should respect and nurture so I can grow as a unique and worthwhile person? *I don't know!*

How could I face the new millennium feeling so inadequate? I had either cut myself off from my internal spiritual resources or else I had none to begin with. And if I had none, I was going to *get* some. This is America, dammit, and if I couldn't find psychic energies for sale somewhere in this penny arcade of a country, I might as well move to Canada where the government would take care of it.

These thoughts were careering through my head as I drove down a busy street one weekend. What to do, what to do? Then—call it coincidence, call it fate, call it a narrative stretch, call it what you want—I passed the Southeast Community Convention and Expo Center Fair Grounds and Raceway. On the marquee outside, sandwiched between notices for the Odd Fellows Awards Dinner and the Pinewood Derby, was listed the big event for this weekend: The South Suburban Solstice Crystal Faire and Spiritual Energy Concordance. "What luck!" I thought as I turned hard and pulled into the parking lot.

CRYSTALS

MOTHER NATURE'S VIBRATORS

FIRST I SHOULD ADMIT that my knowledge of crystal lore was rather sketchy. For example, a heart condition and high blood pressure have forced me to cut salt from my diet, so that widely used crystal isn't part of my life. At one time, however, it left a big impression on me. Growing up in Detroit, we often made school trips to the largest salt mine in America, directly beneath the city. (Remember, too, that the Soviet Union used to send dissidents to work in salt mines in Siberia, so perhaps there *is* a mild therapeutic effect to be had.) Also, I do enjoy an occasional glass of Crystal Light and even Crystal Pepsi, so perhaps I already had a head start.

No wonder we only use it when company comes over.

I paid my admission and strolled the exhibit floor. The place was jumping—well, maybe more like floating. Everyone was in such a wonderful mood, I felt like I was at an Amway awards dinner. The people in the booths were incredibly friendly, and the attendees all seemed to know each other. Everyone was quite happy to tell me everything they knew about the power of crystals. Admittedly, their knowledge was completely intuitive, not based on any scientific data or testing, but I knew that if I relied only on those things that science officially approves, I'd be cutting myself off from some of the most exciting ideas clattering around this fin de siècle.

I was totally unprepared for what I was to discover at the Faire. The crystals they were talking about here weren't salt and sugar, but quartz, azurite, amethyst, and other semiprecious stones. And these crystals, which I'd always associated with yard filler and cheap jewelry, are actually little storehouses of natural psychic energy. Because of their strong, latticelike molecular structure, they act like spiritual batteries, dry cells for parched souls.

All sorts of magical and healing properties are attributed to crystals. They can relieve stress, cure headaches, stimulate dreams, aid intuition, strengthen the immune system, help access the human unconscious, and ultimately prolong life. Before you scoff, think of the example of rich old ladies: They surround themselves with diamonds and Baccarat crystal, and they seem to live for *centuries*.

In addition, I learned that crystals and gemstones all

Beware of Fraud!

Many unscrupulous individuals have climbed aboard the crystal-powered bandwagon and are swindling people with bogus claims for spiritually useless products. The wary consumer should view suspiciously anyone who advocates the beneficial properties of

Highway salt

Celery salt

Cubic zirconium

Crystal methedrine

Crystal radio sets

Crystal Drāno

Billy Crystal

vibrate with their own individual frequency. As someone told me, "This means they have personalities, just like us humans." Some are perky, some are pouty, some are obsessive-compulsive, and so on. You don't just buy any old crystal; you wait for one with a personality you can relate to, one that operates on your own wavelength. You'll know when you find the right one, because when you hold it, you feel like it's been waiting for you all along. This way you'll know you're not getting ripped off by paying big bucks for a common chunk of rock.

At one booth I met Bernardo, who proved to be the most helpful expert on crystalology I found at the Faire. He explained how some crystals contain more power than others, how each is charged up by the individual who uses it, how to cleanse it in a box of sea salt and "rededicate" its energies, and how crystals work best when they are aligned with your seven bodily chakras.

"Crystals can do you a great deal of good while you sleep," Bernardo said. "If they are laid out in a line near your chakras, then as you sleep energy will flow between the crystals and your body." He was very convincing in his argument, but I had no interest in buying his latest product, a nightshirt with seven crystals aligned with chakra points sewn up the back seam.

I told Bernardo about my general spiritual malaise and my doubts that I had any psychic energies to speak of. He assured me that I *must* have those energies, or else I wouldn't be drawn to this type of fair (couldn't argue with that). He then proceeded to outfit me with those crystal products that would clear me of all negative energy and put me back in the pink. I took almost all his suggestions, but I drew the line at the crystal suppositories; they looked *awfully* big for the job. I left the Expo Center and Raceway a few dollars lighter but enthusiastic and expectant of fresh, high-octane spiritual fuel.

Well, I must be doing something wrong because my energy level has not increased, and may even be diminishing. It may have something to do with the physical exertion of wearing almost 30 pounds of quartz on various parts of my body. The quartz prism skullcap was a complete waste of money, since it becomes too hot to wear whenever the sun is out. The amethyst insoles are incredibly painful to walk on, and the rock-crystal candy pendant that I'm supposed to wear around my neck keeps attracting sweat bees. All in all, I feel like I need a vacation.

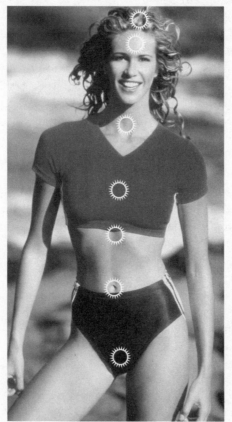

Chakras are points within your body where cosmic energy gathers and makes itself useful to the physical body. There are seven points in the body where chakras are located, as shown in this picture of Elle MacPherson. With or without crystals, she obviously has got her chakras aligned. Hello, nurse!

NATIVE AMERICAN SPIRITUALITY

SWEATIN' TO THE OLDIES

WHAT ABOUT THE LAND? So much of what is being predicted for the end involves earthquakes, floods, tornadoes, and blood raining from the skies—all such terrible shocks to the face of Mother Earth, our nurturer, our friend, our planet. What does she have to say about what will happen?

In 1974, scientists James Lovelock and Lynn Margulis formulated a startling new theory: that our planet is more than just a locale for weather patterns, parking lots, and subdivisions. The earth is really a complex living organism, certainly bigger than any known to us before, which adapts actively to situations and reacts defensively to any threat it perceives. You may have heard of this as the Gaia Hypothesis, named after one of the seemingly innumerable ancient goddesses of the earth.[†] The Gaia Hypothesis states that the earth will regulate herself to cope with the insults we heap upon her, such as strip mines and Disney World. If we pump too much smoke into her air, she'll have a figurative "coughing fit" and respond with acid rain. If we continue dumping toxic pollutants everywhere, she'll open up a hole in the ozone layer to increase our mortality rate until we learn our les-

[†] Though not, as many have asserted, one of the Gabor sisters.

son. If we still don't listen, she'll unleash earthquakes, volcanoes, killer viruses, and polar shifts—quite a tantrum, but isn't that just like a woman?

Ouch! I sincerely and wholeheartedly apologize for that remark. *Now* can you see how confused my energies are? I manage to insult both Mother Earth and half the world's population in a single stroke, and all for an incredibly lame punch line. That's just not like me—honest!

I needed mentors, I could tell. I needed to reconnect to the planet—fast. The people I can think of with the closest connection to the land are the Native Americans. From what little I know about their culture, they have a special love for the planet and respect its needs. To help reinforce this connection, the U.S. government and the rest of society have worked to make sure the natives never have enough opportunities to be tempted to move away from their natural surroundings. With their close connection to Mother Earth, you'd think that Native Americans would know something about the end of it all. And they do.

Long thought to be the most spiritual of Indian tribes because they live in such groovy desert surroundings and make nice pottery, the Hopi have a very articulate view of man's relationship to the earth. According to some, the tribe has also witnessed the destruction of the earth in prehistory—first by ice, then by water (roughly at the same time as Noah and other deluge stories of the Middle East!). During each of these destructions, the Spirit Father assured the Hopi that they would be saved while those around them would perish. The Ant People sequestered these chosen ones safely (if uncomfortably) underground while all the purging was going on. For the destruction by water, the Spirit Father commanded Pöqánghoya and Palöngawhoya, the giant twins who keep the earth rotating on its axis, to leave their posts at the North and South Poles. The world teetered off balance, sending mountains crashing into the ocean and the seas and lakes splashing over onto the land. So the next time you go kicking over anthills, think about what civilization owes to those brave little guys from the past. Think also about the giant ants in the movie *Them!* and remember that those angry arthropods came out of the Arizona desert. Coincidence?

Is this Hopi legend an early account of a polar shift, or merely a modern version cooked up in an ancient language to suggest that the Hopi were somehow aware that the earth is an axially spinning sphere before any other civilization had a clue? We may never know.

A new purification of the earth—this time by fire— is undoubtedly on its way, according to the Hopi. Prophecies say it will be preceded by certain signs: People will build a house and throw it in the sky (Airplanes? Skylab? *The Wizard of Oz?*); cold places will become hot and hot places cold (latest improvements in home heating and cooling?); a blue star will appear in the heavens (Glinda the Good Witch? Howard Stern?).

All this information told me there was precious little time to get my spiritual act together. The thought occurred to me to visit the Hopi in Arizona for more insight and guidance, but I'm not really a hot-weather person. So I began to sniff around my own area for more Native American spiritual resources.

So, once again, as luck or narrative desperation might have it, I was driving by the Off-Ramp Presidential Courtyard Motor Inn one evening when I noticed a flashing marquee sitting near the parking lot. The plastic letters on it read "GET INDIAN SPIRITAULTY TONIT 7." This was just the kind of coincidence keeping me from becoming skeptical about my whole spiritual journey.

Inside, the concierge directed me to the Chester Alan

Arthur Room, where I saw a half-dozen other seekers sitting in a circle in maroon stacking chairs. In the middle of that circle stood an arresting-looking man, with shoulder-length gray hair and a hard yet amused face. He wore a fringed buckskin vest, blue jeans, and a black silk shirt. He beckoned me to come in and "complete the circle," as he said colorfully. The presentation had apparently just begun.

Our session's leader introduced himself as Wally Laughing Star, an elder in the La-Vache-Qui-Rit clan of the Ojibway tribe and a practicing shaman. He explained that in the next two hours, he was going to give us all an introduction to the Native American view of the world and our place in it. Apropos of nothing, he said he'd "achieved sobriety" two years ago, and everyone burst into applause.

Wally Laughing Star gave us a quick tour of earth spirituality from his perspective: how the "Creator Spirit" formed us from clay; how he likes to hear us sing, laugh, and dance; his particular affinity for drumming and tobacco smoke (although it sounds like I'm describing a nightclub, it was very moving at the time). I asked him if it were true, as Bernardo had told me,

Personal portable sweat lodges are still on the drawing board.

that the planet was almost one-third crystal, and how big were these Ant People anyway, but he ignored me. Since he wasn't a Hopi, I cut him some slack.

He stressed the interconnectedness of all life on the planet, in the "circle of creation." I asked him if this was the same thing as the planetary energy grid that I'd read about. He abruptly told me that all my questions would be answered by the end of the night. I asked if that included the Ojibway conception of the end of the world. Wally clapped his hands together and asked, "Okay, who's ready for the sweat lodge? I know I am."

Before the sweat lodge ceremony, we picked animal spirit guides to aid us in our growth. For some reason, the other attendees got to choose their own animals, but Wally insisted that my animal spirit was the porcupine. It wasn't until we dispersed that I noticed in the parking lot a pickup truck with the quills of a fresh roadkill jammed in its headlights (I can only guess whose truck it was, but it had Minnesota plates).

Was Mr. World an early manifestation of what became the Gaia Hypothesis? (Probably not.)

Wally set about erecting a small domed structure made of animal skins, tarp, willow reeds, and nylon rope. He explained that fire safety regulations prevented us from using a real fire and hot rocks for the steam in our lodge. He brought out a portable humidifier and a couple of space heaters to do the job.

How about old silent films? (Now you're really reaching.)

"Unfortunately," he announced, "the hotel has asked that we refrain from disrobing to any great degree because of the Baptist ministers' meeting next door in the Warren G. Harding Room. But we won't let these little inconveniences get in the way of our journey. Enter the sweat lodge, my brothers, and speak your souls freely. Take off your shoes and socks, first."

After about 20 minutes in the sweat lodge, I began to realize that this was a waste of time. I enjoy a good *shvitz* as much as the next person, but fully clothed with a group of strangers, it was beginning to feel like a Mexican bus ride (not to mention smell like one). And every time I asked Wally what to do about my energy levels with the end of the world so close at hand, he looked at me and said that the porcupine learns its lessons by experience, and with its slow wit and prickly personality, is lucky to gain any insight at all. Wonderful poetry, sure, but what did it have to do with me?

By the end of the evening, the only thing I had gathered, besides stares and retching sounds from the ministers standing in the lobby, was that my drumming and chanting days were behind me.

ASTROLOGY

BORN UNDER A BAD SIGN

I WAS BEGINNING TO FEEL cast adrift. I had been roughed up by Native American spirituality, and so, by extension, I felt abandoned by Mother Earth and the Spirit Father as well. Believe me, this was a painful insult. I used to *enjoy* camping; how could I ever show my face in the woods again? Especially to a porcupine.

Rejected by earth, I sought answers high above it. Astrology is possibly the oldest science known to man, and is roughly the third oldest profession. (Tax collection is #2.) But it is very hard to find people these days who have an open mind about it. While some fervently believe our personalities and fates are sealed by planetary positions the moment we pop out of the womb, others believe the idea is utter crap. But the answers are not so cut-and-dried. It's hard to deny that the moon, planets, and stars have an effect on our lives (although no evidence exists). We all know that the appearance of a full moon leads to an increase in crazy activity, police arrests, and emergency room admissions (although statistical analysis has shown this to be a myth). And the alignment of the planets at various times in history has caused great upheavals for the earth (or, as we saw in the previous chapter, not).

Besides which, people with the same birthday exhibit very similar personality traits. I share my birthday with such famous people as Peter Jennings, Michael Jackson, Richard Gere, Ingrid Bergman, and Charlie "Bird" Parker. I'm sure we'd find a lot of traits in common if we were ever to meet for cocktails (except that two of them don't drink, and two of them are dead).

This is not the place, however, for a full-scale debate on the merits of astrology. For our purposes, it's best to swallow it hook, line, and sinker, and then see what this combination of art, science, and 900 numbers has to say about our planet at the year 2000.

As the earth spins on its axis, and as its axis rotates enough to give us the different seasons, our North Pole can serve as a pointer to establish our place in the galaxy. The great constellations, of course, are named for the 12 signs of the zodiac; it is against their backdrop that astrological measurements are made. Since the North Pole has been wagging itself at the constellation Pisces for the past 2,000 years or so, we have fittingly been in a Piscean age. This has been characterized by the appearance of Jesus Christ (whose symbol is the fish), the increasing popularity of water sports, and the successful *Free Willy* movies. But our northerly pointer is now about to move from Pisces into Aquarius, so, as the song goes, "This is the dawning of the Age of Aquarius!"

Age of Aquarius: dawning or drowning?

Aquarius is a bringer of transformation and psychic energy, in contrast to Pisces, a sign full of competition and destruction. As we enter the house of Aquarius, it's said we will enter into an age when our spiritual energy will establish better ways of living on earth. Luckily for this theory, entry into the Aquarian age has no fixed date like New Year's Eve. As a result, over the past century, experts have identified dozens of dates when the age may have actually arrived. But all agree that it is here, even if we can't tell when it came.

What's one of the best ways to celebrate the arrival of the Aquarian age, or to hasten its arrival, in case it's late? Trying out for a part in *Hair,* of course! My heart was filled with anticipation when I learned our local community theater was going to mount a big production of "the American Tribal Love-Rock Musical." I studied the part of Woof night and day. I really thought his character spoke for me. I practiced my dancing, I limbered up my voice, I painted my house neon pink and ultraviolet—I got as far into a 1960s mind-set as possible without moving to Berkeley.

But it all came to zilch. My audition was marvelous, but how naïve I was, to think parts in a play like this would only go to the most talented! The roles of Woof and the other main characters were given to those people who donated the most money to the theater in the past year. This was never stated openly, of course. We also-rans were given other reasons for rejection. But it was a sham. Compared to some of the people who landed leading roles, I know I don't look that bad naked. Pale? Sure. Flabby? Maybe. But "repellent"? It's just politics, like everything else.

TAROT

PICK A CARD, ANY CARD

MY EXPERIENCE WITH THE THEATER left me more hurt than I can say. Now I know what heartbreak actors go through when they don't land a coveted part. Inside them is an aching void they need to fill, and often they turn to arcane studies and spiritualism to find some solace. It's not because these people are inherently unstable, pathetically gullible, perennially idle, or addicted to melodramatic gestures. If Shirley MacLaine had gotten that plum role in *Chitty Chitty Bang Bang,* she might not have become the butt of so many jokes depicting her as a reality-resistant loony bird.

I could feel her pain, though. I really wanted to play the role of Woof. I *needed* to sing "Let the Sunshine In" (not to mention "Ninny-glop gloopy, ninny-nobby nooby, la la la lo lo . . .") and welcome the Age of Aquarius. *Now* what was I going to do? Wait around to try out for *Li'l Abner*? I needed to restore my inner balance, so I did something I'd vowed I never do: I went to have my cards read.

Tonée, the woman who cuts my hair, is very multi-talented. Among her occupations are cloth painting, rattan weaving, Reiki massage, and pet psychology. She also reads the tarot, and has been asking me for the longest time for the chance to do a reading with me. So I called her up and set an appointment for the weekend.

Her basement apartment was quite dark and cozy when I got there. There were many smells in the air, only partially overcome by the sandalwood incense sticks. The decorations were part 1960s retro and part 1990s kitsch (or maybe '60s kitsch and '90s retro—I always get them confused).

Tonée greeted me in her usual bubbly way, as if we hadn't seen each other in years. "I'm so *excited* to do your reading," she said. "Not many people get to see me in two of my different worlds, between cutting and reading, I mean. Sit on the cushion there and take your shoes off." She hustled off into a corner. "I'm going to apologize in advance for the music. Usually I have a George Winston CD that's really good for establishing a reflective atmosphere that allows the cards to speak to us, but I lent it to a client with a codependent weimaraner. And all my other music is kinda . . . wild. Except for this." She held up a Carpenters *Greatest Hits* recording for my approval.

"Well," I said, "you're the professional."

"Now, I have to stop you there," Tonée said, pleasantly but firmly. "I'm just a facilitator. I can't tell you what the cards say; what matters is what they say to *you*. And this is your lucky day. I went on a little splurge today at my favorite store, the Arcana Arcade. You have your choice of *five* different commemorative tarot decks." She showed me a tray with the different decks nicely displayed:

"Klaus" is already feeling pre-millennial jitters.

THE QUEEN of HEELS

The HIGH PRIESTESS

The HAIRDRESSER

❧ **Tarot Barbie.** "Kind of a starter deck for younger girls—I teach card-reading when I baby-sit," explained Tonée.

❧ **Tarot *Friends,*** with all the characters from everyone's favorite sitcom, plus the monkey.

❧ **Tarot Batman,** in dark and brooding deco style for younger boys.

❧ **Tarot Trivial Pursuit,** which comes in handy for long car trips.

❧ **Tarot *90210*.**

For no real reason, I chose the last deck.

Tonée asked me if there was a particular problem I was concerned about or if I just wanted a general reading. I told her, "I think the end of the world as we know it is upon us, and humanity is on the verge of an evolutionary leap into pure spirit, and I am so spiritually malnourished that I may miss the whole thing!"

"Oh, is *that* all?" she said reassuringly. "That shouldn't be any big deal. Let's see what the cards can tell us." She shuffled them reverently and laid them out in a pattern she called the Celtic Cross.

The card in my first position was The Dylan of Swords, with Luke Perry's grinning face on it. Tonée asked, "Do you know what this means?" Before I could answer, she said, "The sword represents adversity, and Dylan is a very high card, a prince, in fact. So you are a brave young prince with a nice haircut, riding forth against a tide of adversity. Yay!"

Well, I couldn't find much fault with that, so I let her go on. The card in my second position was The Mega-Mall. "This indicates how many choices are open to you in your struggle. You are faced with almost endless options here, much more than if this card had been The Strip Mall."

In the third position lay an ominous-looking card: Detox. Tonée said, in a low voice, "This is a card of purification, very powerful. You will have to leave many things behind as you move on your journey. Old ways of thinking, house, car, money, friends—that sort of thing."

I was about to object that this seemed a little extreme, but she was hitting the mark so directly that I held my tongue. This was so exciting! Tonée pointed to the next card: "This is a very intriguing card: The Brenda of Cups. It shows you are someone who is too trusting of people who will do you harm. You are gullible and easily taken advantage of."

"Yes, yes!" I blurted out. "You've got it right, Tonée! Tell me more, hurry!"

She continued through the cards—The Principal, The Brandon of Coins, The Convertible, The Pool Cleaner, and so on—each one hitting closer and closer to the bull's-eye. She said my confusion and apparent emptiness were completely understandable, because momentous events loomed on my horizon. It was a sort of "calm before the storm." My near and far future were greatly dependent on my past, so to really understand what was coming up, Tonée suggested something radical: a daily regimen of past-life regressions that would explore all my previous incarnations on this earth.

I told Tonée that I wasn't really a believer in channeling and reincarnation, but she insisted that it was essential and I was strong enough to know the truth. She gave me a little rundown on the basic regression concept, plus a booklet, "Learning from the Mistakes of Your Past Lives." She was so adamant about it that I finally conceded. What did I have to lose, anyway? She told me to start immediately when I got home, and to start a journal detailing my experiences. By the time the Carpenters were finished singing "Calling Occupants of Interplanetary Craft," our session was done.

REINCARNATION

WHO YOU WAS
IS WHAT YOU IS

LIKE I SAID, I was pretty skeptical about my chances of discovering any past lives. If reincarnation were real, you'd think after only a few go-rounds a person would retain some of the knowledge learned from whole previous life spans, but I was still pretty ignorant. I don't know how to shoe a horse, jar preserves, or hunt mastodons. Sure, I can speak ancient Etruscan and a few lost Aramaic dialects fluently, but I attribute this to growing up in a household that encouraged reading.

So I followed Tonée's advice. One afternoon, I closed the blinds and settled into a comfortable sitting position on the floor. I began to breathe deeply and relax, and set my chakras spinning. Trying to keep images of Mrs. Butterworth bottles out of my mind, I opened the chakra on the top of my head. . . .

My Channeling Journal

SATURDAY: Found myself filled with the spirit of Bonaparte! Very exciting at first, then realized it was not Napoleon himself but his brother Christophe. Still, quite interesting. Constant sibling rivalry grew a little tiresome after a while—man, was this guy jealous of his brother! After military success proved elusive for Christophe, he worked to create a remarkable brandy or an enticing dessert to be remembered by. Unsuccessful on both counts.

SUNDAY: Today got further past in past lives. Channeled the spirit of Lugubrius, a hermit living in the mountains of Turkey in 360 C.E. Not much to say. Liked living alone.

MONDAY: Channeled spirit of a priest in northern France in 998, near the first turning of the millennium! Put in a lot of time warning villagers and peasants that Christ was returning soon and the world was about to end. Quite a bit of trouble when it turned out I was wrong. Angry mob stoned me to death as a heretic. Ouch!

TUESDAY: Went into a slight trance just after lunch and found myself filled with the spirit of Liberace. This fluttery, music-filled sensation was with me only briefly—I'm sure he's in great demand these days—but it moved me enough to spend the whole rest of the day gluing little mirrors and rhinestones to all the furniture in the house. I wish my brother George were here.

WEDNESDAY: My first trans-species channeling! I reached out and somehow caught hold of the spirit of a long-dead dolphin king, Kikki Kiikki Kuk XI. The physical experience was incredible, being able to communicate underwater and feel electrical currents through my skin. However, the intellectual content was sorely lacking. His mind seemed to be a continual loop of: ". . . Must avoid sharks . . . Where's the abalone? . . . Must avoid sharks . . . Boy, those Atlanteans sure were pushy SOBs, glad they're gone . . . Swim swim swim swim . . . Why did those UFOs give us all this information about saving the planet? Don't they know the humans don't listen to us, and we've got no hands to write it all down anyway? . . . I sure could go for some abalone . . . Must avoid sharks . . ."

THURSDAY: Low cloud ceiling today. Channeling might prove
hazardous. Opted to watch Rosie O'Donnell Show.

FRIDAY: Channeled the spirit of Robert Welch, founder of the
John Birch Society—very unpleasant experience. Went on for
hours and hours about what was wrong with this country and how
much better it was before "they" all came over and started to
act like they were Americans. Called a few friends to rant and
rave—must remember to call and apologize next month, after
they've calmed down. Fingers still hurt from typing 108
letters to the editor. Starting to feel foolish.

SATURDAY: Channeled a previous life as a peasant baby in 18th-
century China. Died within two days from dysentery. Just our
luck!

SUNDAY: Getting closer to what I believe are my true roots—
royalty and privilege. Found myself filled with the spirit of
someone calling herself Cleopatra. I was tall and beautiful,
with supple brown skin. I had many enemies. I wielded great
power, and men cowered when confronted with my strength and
beauty. I wore silks and furs, and was a crack shot with a .38
calibre.
    Which was my first clue that something was going wrong. I
looked deeper, past the beauty and strength and fur coats.
    God, how disappointing! I wasn't Cleopatra, Queen of
Egypt. I was Tamara Dobson in Cleopatra Jones, bad, beautiful,
and battling pushers in Harlem. Even though the soundtrack was
mega-funky, and I got to fight Shelley Winters to the death,
it wasn't much consolation.

MONDAY: Very confused. Found myself channeling First Engineer
Kowalsky from Voyage to the Bottom of the Sea. Within minutes,
I was hit over the head with a wrench and knocked cold.

TUESDAY: Back in a historical setting. Rough, beautiful land.
Lots of horses. I'm old, dirty, nearly toothless. I sport a
big bushy beard. I've been a miner out in the wilderness for
many years, and it appears to have affected my sanity a bit.
People call me Dusty, and I'm always spitting tobacco juice
and laughing at my own private jokes. Before my trance is

over, the sheriff deputizes me and puts me in charge of the
jailhouse while he goes out to catch some rustlers. Quite a
satisfying past life.

WEDNESDAY: Find myself in a stifling jungle, wearing tattered
woolen uniform. Carrying rifle with bayonet. I am Japanese,
and feel heartless, vicious, nearly inhuman. Am about to
attack a Red Cross nurse I've tied to a tree when someone who
looks a lot like Gary Cooper shoots me three times and I fall
over dead.

THURSDAY: Whole new historical era, gender, race. I am a Negro
slave woman in Georgia, late 1850s. I'm a house slave and have
to follow every whim of my spoiled young mistress. I speak my
mind to her and am tolerated because of my age, but the young
woman still does whatever she pleases. My mistress wants to
wear a shameless gown to an upcoming party, and won't eat a
proper lunch besides. I tell her, "If you don' care what folks
sez about dis family, Ah does. Ah's done tol' ya an' tol' ya,
you can always tell a lady by the way she eats in front of
folks like a bird, an' Ah ain't aimin' for you to go to Mr.
John Wilkes's an' eat like a field hand an' gobble like a
hog."
    "Fiddle dee dee," she tells me. "Ashley Wilkes told me he
likes to see a girl with a healthy appetite."
    I warn her, "What gentlemen sez an' what they thinks is
two diff'rent things. An' I ain't noticed Mr. Ashley askin'
fo' to marry ya."
    I awake from my trance with a sickening realization. What
I've just channeled is a scene from Gone With the Wind, with
me as Hattie McDaniel.

FRIDAY: Furious with the disappointing results of the past few
days' channeling. After my trance, I immediately storm into
the office of David O. Selznick and complain about being cast
in all these tasteless, clichéd roles. The studio chief fires
back at me, "You're lucky to be working at all. I could go out
and shake a tree and find someone to replace you. You're not
the only schmuck in Hollywood, you know. . . ."

I think I'll just quit right now.

The Biblical Apocalypse

Fun with Fundamentalism

I WAS REALLY AT THE END of my rope now. My foray into the esoteric arts had been completely fruitless. As men delivered a fresh truckload of quartz crystals to my driveway, I realized I was no closer to the real truth than when I started. I was closer to bankruptcy and emotional exhaustion, but not to the end of the world.

What could I do now? I knew something *big* was going to happen, but what was it? More important, when would it happen? This obsession and gnawing sense of dread were becoming hazardous to my health—lost sleep, near-miss car accidents, well-meaning threats from family and friends. If our world didn't end at the turn of the century, I (not to mention millions of others) was going to be utterly heartbroken.

Only one resource remained untried. An ancient tome packed with so much destruction, mayhem, payback, and pestilence that it makes every other doomsday book seem like *The Poky Little Puppy*. If you want to know anything about the beginning of the world, the end of the world, or anything in between, this is the place to find it. Few written records have such a nice feeling of closure. I'm talking, of course, about the Holy Bible.

This scriptural research is sort of terra incognita for me. My upbringing in Catholicism did not actively encourage personal Bible study; other people were paid to do that, and my job was to do what they said. In the intervening years, I haven't explored the book much, because of society's rampant secular humanism and the arrival of cable TV in my area. Also, for a while there, some of the Bible's most public spokesmen kept getting caught *in flagrante debimbo*, which did a lot for me professionally but not spiritually. But now my options were running out.

At the very start, I was faced with an important question: Should the Bible be taken as the literal, unerring word of God in any and all matters? My rational side would say no, but I abandoned that part of my brain about three chapters ago. Besides, so much has been written about the Bible and its sources that it would take years just to scratch the surface. Huge amounts of time, money, and effort would be needed for a divinity degree (except the mail-order kind), and the year 2000 is mere months away. I think I'll take the Bible literally and sort out the details later.

This seems as good an excuse as any for biblical inerrancy. Analysis can wait for all the Monday-morning quarterbacks and post-apocalypse experts. The time for action is now!

HAS GOD DESTROYED THE EARTH BEFORE?

EVEN THOUGH WIDESPREAD planetary devastation makes permanent records a little hard to come by, catastrophes have been a constant occurrence over the life of the earth. But this is God's prerogative. After all, if you take the Bible literally, like I do, it shows that God loves the world so much that he created it not once but twice (Gen. 1 and 2:4–23)! It's certainly his privilege to destroy it any way he likes—floods, earthquakes, throw rugs, pudding storms, whatever.

If you're a fundamentalist and believe that the earth is only 6,000 years old, you're left with a very narrow window for any great amount of worldwide destruction. But you still can enjoy that most familiar of catastrophes, the Great Flood. More than ever, there is a big interest today in uncovering the remains of Noah's Ark in the mountains of Turkey. To do so, presumably, would prove that you could fit enough animals❢ into a tri-level gopherwood barge (plus enough food and shovels) that measured

❢ "Seven pairs of all clean animals, the male and its mate; and a pair of the animals that are not clean, the male and its mate; and seven pairs of the birds of the air also" (Gen. 7:2–3). Scholars say the extra animals were inserted in later versions of Genesis to show that Noah was able to make the proper burnt sacrifices to God. (It likely was a good way to keep the other animals in line as well.)

roughly 150 yards long by 25 yards wide by 15 yards high. But the usefulness of this info may be best left to zookeepers and wildlife managers.

More important, to find Noah's Ark would prove the literal truth of the Bible. This would also mean that God created the universe in six days, woman was really made from man's rib, humans and monkeys are not kissin' cousins, and the world will end exactly as described in the Book of Revelation. Whether this is a thing truly to be wished for, we will soon see.

Who went standby?

The Great Flood is not strictly a Judeo-Christian-Islamic concept (the Koran also mentions Noah). Many other cultures tell of large-scale inundations and the re-population of the earth, although among Middle Eastern societies there is no evidence of ancient worries over a possible "ark gap":

Assyrian-Babylonian: Khasisatra, along with his family and servants, piloted a vessel filled with domestic and wild animals, while it rained for six days and nights and "the corpses of the drowned floated like seaweed." Their ark landed on Mount Nizar, after which "Khasisatra and his wife henceforward were granted to live like gods," perhaps because the servants now knew they could be replaced.

Indian: The Mahabharata tells the story of Manu, who spared the life of a fish and was told to build a ship and attach it to the fish's horn. (Skeptical of a connection be-

Rapture:
Watch the Skies!

Many fundamentalists believe that, before all the real
trouble starts at the end, true Christians will be
spared and "raptured." They base this on the writings
of Paul:

> For the Lord himself . . . will descend from
> heaven, and the dead in Christ will rise first. Then
> we who are alive, who are left, will be caught up
> in the clouds together with them to meet the Lord
> in the air; and so we will be with the Lord forever
> (I Thess. 4:16-17).

This heavenly reprieve will result in thousands of persons flying bodily into the air, à la Peter Pan and
Wendy. (If this strikes you as silly, other people explain that true Christians will merely vanish without
warning.)

One can imagine the chaos this will cause on our
highways and in our airports (you won't notice much
difference on Amtrak), not to mention the insurance
headaches that will follow. To date, no underwriter is
offering "Rapture insurance." Still, if you notice the
sky filled with flying humans and you don't live in Me-
tropolis or Gotham City, getting a check for a smashed
windshield might be the least of your problems.

On the other hand, some have argued that the rapture of the truly Christ-like happened long ago, leaving the rest of us to squabble, cheat, oppress, and
kill each other. Can't argue with that.

tween fish and horns? Try looking at a picture of Dizzy Gillespie without thinking of a blowfish.) After the deluge, the fish pulled Manu's boat to Mount Himavat, where Manu was granted a young woman with whom to repopulate the earth (it's a dirty job, but . . .).

Persian: Yima, his wife, and a thousand other couples, along with animals and birds, waited out floods, fires, and earthquakes in an underground fortress "three stories deep with wide avenues," sort of a mega-mall for salvation. Yima and his followers made sure their pleasure dome contained "no evil people, persons with uneven teeth, or lepers," which would eliminate the need for security guards, orthodontists, and dermatologists. There was, however, an Orange Julius stand.

Lithuanian: A flood and windstorm lasted 12 days and nights, forcing a small group of humans and some animals to a high mountaintop. When the waters rose to engulf even the mountain, the Supreme Being, who at the time was munching on giant nuts (a fitting thing for a Supreme Being to do), dropped a shell. The people and animals used the shell to sail to safety, while praising the sloppy personal habits of the Supreme Being.

Aztec-Toltec: A patriarch named Coxcox and his wife, children, and animals set out on a large cypress raft to survive a flood that covered the earth for 52 years. During that time, "all mankind drowned or changed into fish," so no one was left to make fun of the patriarch's name.

Huron: The Great Father of the Indian Tribes gathered his wife, family, and animals onto a large raft to make it through a several-month flood. During the trip, the animals kvetched, whined, and fought constantly. As a punishment, when the raft landed, the Great Father stripped the animals of their power of speech, and was immediately besieged by picketers from PETA.

For all these nations, the flood meant death to evildoers, i.e., their enemies, and salvation and paradise for the good, i.e., themselves. As we have already seen, this "us vs. them" motif is important to keep in mind when talking about the apocalypse.

Could all this mean the flood in Genesis was an actual "earth trauma," possibly caused by the sinking of Atlantis, the passing of an asteroid, or a shift in the earth's geographic poles? To argue against this would mean that enough water erupted on the earth—through rain and from "the fountains of the great deep"—to cover *at least* Mount Ararat (16,945 feet high) and then somehow evaporated or subsided. So I say sure, why not? Let's say it was all real and an earth trauma and the poles did their version of the Electric Slide, and move on.

KEEPS GOING, AND GOING, AND GOING...

THE OLD TESTAMENT prophets (Jeremiah, Ezekiel, Obadiah, et al.) generally spent their time haranguing the Jews about their reprobate ways. Since this sinfulness didn't set off worldwide destruction, as it had in Noah's time, it would appear the Almighty's trigger finger had grown less itchy over the years. In their descriptions of how Jerusalem and anyone caught moping nearby would be destroyed for their sins, the prophets described the same disciplinary methods—earthquakes, plagues, rivers of blood—that come up again in the Book of Revelation. As they used to say in vaudeville, you go with what works.

If you think this outfit is revealing, read on.

The most apocalyptic writer among the prophetic crowd was Daniel of lion's-den fame. While the first half of the Book of Daniel is fit for Sunday school, the second has had people running for shelter at least since the time of Jesus.

Daniel is a favorite among end-of-the-world types, and not just for his vivid imagery. He is also specific about dates, if still vague about what those dates will witness. In one vision, Daniel watches a goat with immense horns sweep angels and stars from the sky and trample them underfoot. The roguish ram even disrupts the burnt offerings in the sanctuary. This sorry situation goes on for 2,300 evenings and mornings, after which "the sanctuary shall be restored to its rightful state" (8:14).

Now, right there in the Book of Daniel, the angel Gabriel identifies this vision as "the appointed time of the end" and the goat as the king of Greece. So when the king of Greece is defeated, the sanctuary will be restored, i.e., Jerusalem will be free, and that will be that. As you might expect, the 2,300 days have since come and gone. But that hasn't stopped thinkers of many persuasions from puzzling out this vision. It inspired William Miller to predict the end in 1844, thus giving birth to the Seventh-Day Adventists, and such inspiration continues to the present time. After all, who knows how long a "day" might be? It was only centuries later that the Teamsters and other unions provided an answer.

In another passage, Daniel is told that 70 weeks will pass between the reestablishment of Jerusalem after the Babylonian captivity and the eventual destruction of the Holy City (which to the proper mind-set means the destruction of the world). Seventy weeks equals 490 days, which the Essenes at Qumran took to mean 490 years, which is why they were hiding out in caves in the first century C.E., awaiting the end of the world and misplacing what have come to be known as the Dead Sea Scrolls.❡

Finally, Daniel has a wide-screen, Cinerama-type vision of a calamitous battle between armies of the north and the south. After this battle will come the final judgment, when the dead shall rise and God shall dole out

---

❡ What will archaeologists find in the shelters of today's millennial survivalists? Copies of *Soldier of Fortune*, *Hustler*, and *The Turner Diaries*? Hardly the stuff of legend, but history is rarely tidy.

Catholics Still Roamin'

What?! The largest denomination in Christianity won't get to join in the apocalypse? Sad but true. The Roman Catholic church has officially stated the end of the world is not—repeat, not—at hand. Pilgrimages to Rome and Jerusalem are expected to increase in the year 2000, which John Paul II has declared a jubilee year (after the Old Testament idea of a special year when debts are forgiven and wrongs righted), but everyone has been advised to book a return ticket. For those Catholics who still want to cover their bets, here are a few patron saints whose protective intervention may prove useful. If we're lucky, the plague will play a major role in the end, so we'll have plenty of saints to intercede for us:

EARTHQUAKE: Saint Emygdius

EXPLOSIONS: Saint Barbara

FAMINE: Saint Conrad

FIRE: Saint Catherine of Siena

FLOODS: Saint Columban

HOPELESS CAUSES: Saint Jude

LOST KEYS: Saint Zita

OVERSLEEPING: Saint Vitus

PILGRIMS: Saint Benedict Labre

PLAGUE: Saint Casimir, Saint Edmund, Saint Elizabeth of Hungary, Saint Geneviève, Saint Godeberta, Saint Gregory the Great, Saint Leocadia, Saint Rock, Saint Sebastian, Saint Ursula, Saint Walburga

the eternal rewards and damnations. And when might that be?

> From the time that the regular burnt offering is taken away and the abomination that desolates is set up, there shall be one thousand two hundred ninety days. Happy are those who persevere and attain the thousand three hundred thirty-five days (12:11-12).

666

Stay off highways wherever you see this sign. It's a prank, or something worse. The Interstate Highway Commission has assured us there is no Route 666 anywhere in the United States, and if there were, they wouldn't tell the public about it.

The puzzled expression you are currently wearing was probably reflected in Daniel's own face, because God tells him to go lie down and not worry about it.

While the ancient Jews would have understood the symbols employed by Daniel in his visions, we modern readers would need advanced degrees to keep our Medeans straight from our Moabites. So were Daniel's visions accurate prophecy? Did he correctly predict, however floridly, the winners of the big battles between north and south? Yes and no. Evidence exists that a portion of this eponymous book was written 300 years *after* Daniel's time, when Judea was occupied by the Greek army. The predictions in Daniel are astoundingly correct up to events in 167 B.C.E., then go astoundingly wrong, beginning with the surprise victory of the rebel Maccabees over the Greeks, which Daniel somehow failed to foresee. It would appear that Daniel's prophecies (which were written in Hebrew) were added to the rest of his book (written in Aramaic) to give courage to the Jews during this foreign persecution. Such pre-dating is common in both prophecy (see St. Malachy) and tax fraud.

Apocalyptic literature like the Book of Daniel was very popular among the Jews from around 200 B.C.E.. to

100 C.E. Roughly 300 different books and letters survive that tell how, after a time of intense suffering, God will crush the forces of evil, reward the good, and establish an earthly paradise. These were meant to give courage to the Jews during rough times. The early Christians, in their times of persecution, wanted one of these ripping yarns for their own, and so they got the Book of Revelation.

DRAGONS, BEASTS, AND NAUGHTY LADIES

THE REVELATION OF St. John the Divine is arguably the most controversial book presently included in either the Old or New Testament. Through time, just about every major figure in church history, from Gaius to Martin Luther, has taken a turn at slamming it (Luther flatly stated that "the Holy Spirit had nothing to do with its composition").

Why such a hostile reaction? It could mean that Revelation is difficult to comprehend. It could arise from misuse of the book by different churches and sects. It could mean the book is a bunch of Technicolor horse-shit. However, the contrarian in me (not to mention the conspiracist) likes to think that all this controversy proves that the book contains important information that some figures in authority would rather not talk about.

Scholars likewise dispute whether the John who wrote this work (aka St. John the Divine) is the same as the Apostle John. Popular tradition holds this to be the case. Popular tradition also says that St. John the Divine survived immersion in boiling oil under Roman torture; was once handed a cup of poison, blessed the drink, and watched as the poison exited the cup in the form of a serpent; and at the hour of his death, dug a grave in the shape of a cross, laid himself down in it, and in a blinding flash of light disappeared completely. So we're going along with tradition on this one.

The problem of the "single John" theory arises from the difference in writing styles between the two books. While the Gospel of John is written in lyrical and flawless Greek, Revelation is crammed full of grammatical errors, poor word choices, and general "barbarisms" (a word Greek scholars attach to most things they don't like). If the average reader could compare the original writing, according to these arguments, the books clearly would be as dissimilar as *The New Yorker* and *The National Enquirer*. But who cares about scholarship when we're talking about the end of the world here? Buncha eggheads.

Revelation was written between 64 and 96 C.E., while some John or other lived on the Greek island of Patmos. The book is a letter to seven fledgling churches in Asia Minor. John begins with some pleasantries, then insists that Jesus himself brought him the vision he is about to relate (a claim of divine authority that no other book of the New Testament feels compelled to make). After some kind words, the churches are berated for their failings—adultery, heresy, and being lukewarm—and treated to some contemporary gossip.

It's hard to keep a good saint down.

Then the good stuff starts.

John looks up from his writing tablet to see a door ajar in heaven. Through it he can see the Almighty seated on his throne. God is green and red in color, while his throne is surrounded by an emerald rainbow and a sea of glass—a rather festive, Christmas-y picture, although it would be many centuries before the first Neiman-Marcus catalog. Around the throne are four creatures, something like a lion, an ox, a human, and an eagle. They are hard to make out, since each is covered with eyes in front and back.[❜]

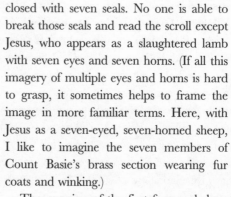

The Almighty holds a scroll in his hand, securely closed with seven seals. No one is able to break those seals and read the scroll except Jesus, who appears as a slaughtered lamb with seven eyes and seven horns. (If all this imagery of multiple eyes and horns is hard to grasp, it sometimes helps to frame the image in more familiar terms. Here, with Jesus as a seven-eyed, seven-horned sheep, I like to imagine the seven members of Count Basie's brass section wearing fur coats and winking.)

The opening of the first four seals heralds the arrival of the Four Horsemen of the Apocalypse—War, Famine, Pestilence, and Death. When Famine appears, voices in heaven shout, "A quart of wheat for a day's pay, and three quarts of barley for a day's pay, but do not damage the olive oil and the wine!" (6:6) (don't be surprised to hear this motto on more and more people's lips in coming years). The heavenly equestrians are then given authority to kill a quarter of the world's population, which they promptly proceed to do.❜❜

Jorge, the fifth horseman?

When the fifth seal is broken, the martyrs of the

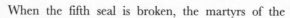

[❜] Before describing the vivid images in the book any further, I should point out that John wrote the book without the aid of hallucinogens, lava lamps, or electric lyres.

^{❜❜} Is it any coincidence for our times that Notre Dame's Four Horsemen of football fame are all dead today? Probably not, because if they weren't, they'd be very, very old.

faith begin screaming for their deaths to be avenged. Instead of a divine rebuke to mind their own business (which, if this were the God of the Old Testament, would have been the least of their problems), they are each given a white robe and told to be patient, just like at the pool at the Beverly Hills Hilton.

The breaking of the sixth seal is a real blowout. Earthquakes. Eclipses. The moon turning red. "The stars of the sky fell to the earth as the fig tree drops its winter fruit when shaken by a gale. The sky vanished like a scroll rolling itself up, and every mountain and island was removed from its place" (6:13–14). Depending on your perspective, this description could fit a nuclear strike, a polar shift, a meteor shower, or Gaia shaking her skin like a wet dog to rid herself of those pesky humans messing with her ecosystems. In any event, it means overtime for everyone at CNN.

Then the commotion stops, and angels place seals on the foreheads of the elect 144,000—12,000 people from each of the 12 tribes of Israel. These will enter into a blissful existence in heaven.❡

"When the Lamb opened the seventh seal, there was silence in heaven for about half an hour" (8:1). But this little intermission offered no rest, except for a brief opportunity to stand in the lobby and sip warm

❡ This is not wonderful news for those of us alive today, statistically speaking. During John's lifetime, the population of the earth was approximately 200 million; today it is 5.8 billion. So the chance of any of us being included in this exclusive group has shrunk from 1 in 1,387 to 1 in 40,278.

The only defense is God's seal, or a nice pilot's cap.

Will The Real Antichrist
Please Stand Up?

Althought the word Antichrist never appears in the Book of Revelation, it is tossed around freely by end-times watchers and other people with limited vocabularies. Throughout history, many people have suffered the slander of being identified as the Son of Perdition, but the passage of time has let most of them off the hook. Is there anything we can learn from a partial roster of people accused of being the A.C.?

- Nero, the most likely candidate for the Beast in Revelation, since the numerical values of letters in his name in Greek and Hebrew add up to 666

- Muhammad

- Attila the Hun

- Most of the popes, especially since the Protestant Reformation (and, by extension, Catholics in general)

- Martin Luther (included in the spirit of ecumenism)

- French and English intellectuals during the American Revolution, for espousing deism

- Napoléon Bonaparte, for trying to forge an updated Roman Empire

- Benito Mussolini, ditto

- Adolf Hitler, mega ditto

- Franklin Delano Roosevelt, for numerological reasons and autocratic leadership style (although the Bible makes no mention of fireside chats or Scottish terriers)

- Francisco Franco (and now, because of his lineage, the famous and charismatic King Juan Carlos of Spain)

- Mikhail Gorbachev (being Russian was bad enough, but the forehead splotch?)

- John F. Kennedy (since he was a Catholic and thus would be taking his orders from a resurrected Roman Empire)

- Henry Kissinger, for working for peace in the Middle East and for that heavy accent

- Saddam Hussein (although he's had competition for the title from Khadafy, Arafat, and the Ayatollah Khomeini, being from Babylon is a dead giveaway)

- Prince Bernhard of the Netherlands (it's hard to imagine a list of powerful world figures without him)

- The European Common Market computer in Brussels, nicknamed "the Beast" by staffers

- A computer program run by Al Gore (an assertion made recently and ironically on the World Wide Web)

- Aleister Crowley (self-confessed, so it probably doesn't count)

- The Beatles (their press agent reportedly boasted, "They're completely Antichrist")

- John Lennon, for all the subversive, one-world messages he sent out in songs like "Imagine"

- Johnny Rotten (also self-confessed)

- Someone at Procter & Gamble, because of the moon and stars in the corporate symbol

- Teenage Mutant Ninja Turtles (while not really the Antichrist, these cartoon figures are doing work in A.C.'s name)

- Barney the Dinosaur (almost goes without saying)

- Episcopalians, Presbyterians, and Methodists, according to Pat Robertson, anyway. When discussing ecumenism on the air on January 14, 1991, the televangelist and statesman wannabe revealed, "You say, 'You're supposed to be nice to the Episcopalians and the Presbyterians and the Methodists, and this, that, and the other thing.' Nonsense! I don't have to be nice to the spirit of the Antichrist."

- Pat Robertson, determined to be the Antichrist by end-times researcher Constance Cumbey because of his Middle East interests and smooth TV manner. Cumbey dropped the assertion when Robertson threatened to sue, so I guess he's not really the Son of Perdition.

Of course, all such speculation about who is really the Antichrist could just be a Mickey Mouse occupation. Then again...

Chardonnay. John watched as seven angels armed themselves with trumpets—and, as some of you might know, biblical trumpets, unlike those in a bullfight, are generally not good portents. We'll skip the details of what happens when the trumpets sound. Suffice it to say there's a lot of horrible carnage of a planet-wide nature.

Those who see parallels between modern warfare and the Book of Revelation gain a lot of "ammunition" from chapters 8 and 9. From a bottomless pit emerge swarms of super-locusts that torture anyone who doesn't wear God's seal on the forehead. The bugs "were like horses equipped for battle," with human faces, scales like breastplates, and wings that sounded like chariots rushing into battle. A spiteful portrayal of the Roman soldiers who destroyed Jerusalem's Second Temple? An approximate description of an attack helicopter or a cruise missile (at least without the part about "hair like women's hair")? Possibly, but to paraphrase Freud, sometimes a crown-wearing, longhaired, big-toothed flying scorpion is just a . . . well, you get the picture.

After more noise and destruction, John is handed a scroll by a gigantic angel and told to eat it, something we can all relate to, especially the Grateful Dead fans among us. "It will be bitter to your stomach, but sweet as honey

Go Philly!

The only American city mentioned in either the Old or New Testament is Philadelphia (Rev. 3:7)! Okay, John is talking about the Philly that is in Asia Minor, not Pennsylvania, but I think the citizens of the City of Brotherly Love should still feel some hometown pride!

in your mouth" (10:9). Ever the good sport, John does as he's told. As if he needed any boost to his imagination, after this bittersweet treat, his visions are even more wild. In fact, the remainder of the book contains too many details to examine here. For clearer organization, let's concentrate on the cast of characters that are very familiar to end-times devotees: the Dragon, the Beast, the Second Beast (or the False Prophet), and the Whore of Babylon.

The Dragon: The Dragon is introduced waiting to gobble up the baby being born to a woman floating in the sky. It's your classic dragon, red with seven heads and ten horns with a crown on each head. (Again with the horns? Okay, how about seven kids at a birthday party at Burger King, with three members of Basie's brass section.) John identifies the dragon directly as Satan, but some clever commentators insist that it must be Communist China. (Editorial cartoons must be postgraduate-level reading for some of these thinkers.)

The Beast: While the Dragon looks on, the Beast rises up from the sea to begin its mischief. "On its horns were ten diadems, and on its heads were blasphemous names." The Beast has a body like a leopard's, feet like a bear's, and a mouth like a lion's. And, as with any other

No matter how good an interest rate they may be charging, think twice before signing up for any kind of card like this.

pop sensation, the people go nuts over the thing. It is prone to uttering haughty and blasphemous words, that saucy thing, and throws its weight around for 42 months—precisely the amount of time between the release of the Beatles' "I Want to Hold Your Hand" and *Sgt. Pepper's Lonely Hearts Club Band.* Coincidence?

The False Prophet: Then from the ground rose another beast, with two horns like a lamb and a voice like the Dragon's. This one works as an advance man and spin doctor for the real Beast, arranging special events and photo ops to boost the Beast's credibility. Their performance is so masterful (despite damaging exposés in *The Star*) that everyone on earth eventually worships the Beast. Soon they create the one fashion accessory no one can do without: the Number of the Beast, 666.

This is a number I'm sure you've heard a lot about. Its evil is emphasized by the fact that it comes short of the mystical, all-important number 7—three different times, no less. Throughout history, many have tried to determine whose name is represented by the three sixes ("This calls for wisdom: let anyone with understanding calculate the number of the beast, for it is the number of a person"—13:18). So far it is still up for debate, although John Tesh comes close. Superstition about the triple six is widespread even today. For example, skyscrapers with a 666th floor usually label it 667.

Everyone will be required to wear the 666 on their right hands or their foreheads, because without it no one

will be able to buy or sell goods. It will be much more important than an import-export license or even an ATM card. Many end-times watchers insist that the mark will be a tattooed bar code, or else a microchip implanted under the skin at birth. Others think it might be something less complicated, such as a credit card accepted everywhere or a designer baseball cap. ❦

❦ My advice for avoiding this problem is to watch out for anyone who wants you to tattoo a bar code or a 666 on your head. Be suspicious of such people. They might be up to something.

Angels at 12 O'Clock!

For those readers who are enjoying and participating in the current popularity of angels, the Book of Revelation may be somewhat of a shock. These end-times angels are not concerned with any "positive thinking" or "life-affirming creativity" on your part. Here they are God's enforcers—single-minded, destructive, ruthless. (This doesn't mean we should confuse them with Jesuits, however.) Be careful if you have a vision of an angel who is about to spill the contents of a bowl on your head. Chances are you haven't won the Super Bowl and it's not Gatorade.

Jesus is not thrilled with this beastly banking activity, and so assembles his 144,000-member virgin army (who are probably a lot tougher than they sound) with the mark of the Almighty on *their* foreheads to do battle. And while seven angels pour out plagues on the earth from big bowls, the forehead forces assemble for the final battle at Armageddon. This locale is generally taken to mean the hills outside the Israeli city of Megiddo. Depending on your source, Megiddo is either a strategically important city that has been the site of many ancient battles or a ditchwater flyspeck of no value whatsoever. For centuries, the Megiddo Chamber of Commerce has been trying to figure out how to capitalize on their notoriety to attract small businesses and retirees, without much luck.

The Whore of Babylon. John is whisked away from the battle by an angel and shown a woman in the wilderness, clothed in purple and scarlet and fine jewels. Her identity is really no secret, since on her forehead is written "Babylon the Great, Mother of Whores and of Earth's Abominations."

HELLO!
My Name Is...

BABYLON THE GREAT, MOTHER OF WHORES

Who are you?

HELLO!
My Name Is...

AND OF EARTH'S ABOMINATIONS

Who are you?

(Luckily, like at a Shriner's convention, name tags are readily available throughout this book.) And she is such big-time trouble that all of chapter 18 is a song detailing how hard she'll be whacked for her iniquities. It is indeed unfortunate that there are so few major roles for women in this apocalyptic story, and that the most significant one is of a "hooker with a heart of gold" (though not gold in a good way). This same problem exists in Hollywood today, but on the bright side, such roles often lead to Oscar nominations.

The Whore (or Hoor, in Canadian translations) is "sitting on a scarlet beast that was full of blasphemous names, and it had seven heads and ten horns" (17:3). (Back to the Burger King image.) The seven heads represent the mountains where the Whore sits—the seven hills of Rome—as well as seven kings, "of whom five have fallen, one is living, and the other has not yet come; and when he comes, he must remain only a little while" (17:10). The beast itself is also a king, but to avoid confusion we'll let that pass for the moment. The ten horns are

> ten kings who have not yet received a kingdom, but they are to receive authority as kings for one hour, together with the beast. These are united in yielding their power and authority to the beast; they will make war on the Lamb, and the Lamb will conquer them (17:12-14).

I hope this is clear enough for you.

Back to the battle. The Beast and False Prophet are defeated by Jesus and "thrown alive into the lake of fire that burns with sulfur." Then an angel brings a chain down from heaven, binds up the Dragon for 1,000 years, and tosses him into the bottomless pit. Now Jesus reigns over a blessed earth for 1,000 years, which many people take to be the real Millennium. After this, the Dragon is freed again, carnage ensues, and eventually all souls are judged and end up in heaven or in the lake of fire.

The remainder of the Book of Revelation is a description of an earthly paradise called the New Jerusalem. While its physical descriptions would be of interest to architects and civil engineers, I won't go into details now. We certainly have enough images to chew on. And I left out most of the real gory parts.

To those who study the subject academically, St. John the Divine's writing is meant to show that Rome will suffer revenge for its persecution of the Jews and that emerging Jewish sect, the Christians. The book is a sort of pep talk to the frightened followers in Asia Minor, the language made poetic to shield them from possible harm from the authorities. "Babylon," an ancient tormentor of the Jews, is a code for a corrupt world power, in this case imperial Rome. The beast is almost certainly that fat tyrant Emperor Nero. Most early Christians believed Jesus's Second Coming was going to occur within the lifetimes of those who knew him personally, so to get them through the dark nights, it was only natural they would want an apocalyptic book of their own, giving the play-by-play of who gets what from whom and how hard.

"Rats! They've figured it out! Maybe if I shave the mustache..."

To those among us who don't believe in splitting hairs, the Babylon in the Book of Revelation is Babylon, that is, Iraq and Saddam Hussein. And everything in Revelation will happen—or is happening this very minute—exactly as it is written. While John may have used some fanciful imagery, he only did this because he was describing things unknown to his first-century mind—atomic explosions, attack helicopters, asteroid showers, supermarket scanners. But even he knew that Babylon is Babylon, a beast is a beast, and a whore is a whore.

So, dear reader, where do you stand on the issue? Is the Book of Revelation an interesting historical document particular to a place and era, or is it a blow-by-blow transcript of humanity's impending doom?

Okay, wise guy, let me phrase it this way: At the end of the century, would you rather be sitting in the comfort of your living room, cracking jokes with your wise-guy friends, or would you rather be digging drainage ditches for your survival shelter deep in the woods, getting used to the taste of K rations and boiled coyote, and waiting for the end of the world to come?

Aha! I *thought* so.

Apocryphal Apocalypses

Many other writings describing the end times were written around the time of Christ but early on were omitted from the Christian church canon. In the centuries since, almost all evidence of the following writings has been destroyed:

The Revelation to Binky

The Revelation of Thinner Thighs in 30 Days

The Letter from an Undergraduate at a Large Midwestern University (also known as "The Lab Partner Debauchery")

The Book of Virtues

The Book Where We Win and They Lose

The Book of the Big, Scary End

LOOKIN' FOR CLUES

MY VISIT WITH JOHN EASTER YOUTHBONE

I WAS AT THE BREAKING POINT. My head was full to exploding with images of blood, plagues, bottomless pits, and horse-sized locusts. I don't know what I expected to find when I cracked open Revelation, but now I was more agitated than ever. I needed to clear my head, so I jumped in the car and hit the road.

I headed out past the city limits and the chaos of all the humanity. It was a clear, black, moonless night. As I gazed up at the stars, I wondered whether they were fixed in their places, or whether the whole glittering gallery would come unstuck and pelt the earth like overripe produce. What did it matter if it happened from a nudge from God or an unstable polar cap? The result would be the same.

I headed farther and farther out into the plains. Traffic was extremely light—a few trucks and cars, but very far between. Where was everybody? Raptured? Did I miss the Rapture somehow? Or were the Bulls playing on TV? Each explanation was as plausible as the next. But such relativism ate away at me inside. There could be nothing *relative* about the end of the world. I needed some solid answers before my fears and intuitions drove me insane. I compulsively punched the radio button, trying to find something that didn't set me on edge.

Punch. ". . . tell all those pinheads in Washington that if they think we're stupid . . ."

Punch. ". . . more more music and less less talk! More more more . . ."

Punch. ". . . coach says we have to cut down on mistakes, but I don't think we . . ."

Punch. "Here's a news flash: Noah's Ark has been found!"

Punch. ". . . mas mas musica y menos menos hablar! Mas mas mas . . ."

What? Wait a minute! Backup scan! How do I backup scan with this thing? Lousy factory-installed . . .

"That's right, friends. Out of the mountains of Turkey comes news of the discovery of the century, or really the discovery of the millennium. Noah's Ark—which many people have been calling merely a myth or a child's bedtime story—the actual ark used by Noah has been discovered in the Ararat Mountains of eastern Turkey, near the Iranian border. Buried for centuries beneath snow and ice, the floating sanctuary has been found by a joint team from the United States, Russia, and France."

I couldn't believe my ears were hearing this news, right when I needed it most. Was it coincidence? Revelation? A taped rerun?

"Of course, no photos have been released," the resonant voice continued. "All evidence of the discovery has been suppressed to avoid massive panic among the peoples of the world. Because if the story of Noah and the ark turns out to be true, friends, then everything else in the Bible must be absolutely true as well. Adam and Eve. The virgin birth. And most important, the coming of the Antichrist. And the Powers That Be don't want you to know about it. It would disrupt their tidy plan for world domination."

Was the Gipper Really the Antichrist?

You know, I turn back to your ancient prophets in the Old Testament and the signs foretelling Armageddon and I find myself wondering if—if we're the generation that is going to see that come about. I don't know if you've noted any of those prophecies lately, but believe me they certainly describe the times we're going through. —October 18, 1983

To many of us, it seemed like a miracle that the presidency of Ronald Reagan didn't end up inciting Armageddon. Handing over control of America's nuclear arsenal to a doddering, manipulable B movie actor could've ended the world in a Technicolor blast, but somehow we're still here. What does this seeming impossibility all mean? Is there more to this man than Teflon and pomade?

· Add up the letters in his full name—Ronald Wilson Reagan—and what do you get? No, not 18—666!

· He survived an assassination attempt, fulfilling Rev. 13:3, "One of its heads seemed to have received a death-blow, but its mortal wound had been healed."

· When Reagan and his charming, astrology-dependent wife, Nancy, retired to California, the street number of their new home was 666! They had it changed, of course, but the post office still knew where to deliver his mail.

Now that the former president's mind has succumbed to illness, and his influence is fading fast, we are faced with the question: Was he really the Antichrist, or was he just married to it?

What had I found? Who was this guy?!

"In other end-times news, floods in India, earthquakes in China, volcanoes in Tahiti, and hailstones the size of bowling balls in Saskatchewan. Details at the top of the hour. You're listening to WWEA, End-Times Radio, with your host, John Easter Youthbone. Back in a minute."

Then there followed an ad for a special sale on canned goods, bottled water, and air purifiers at the local do-it-yourself store.

In the dark expanses of the Midwest prairie, this voice rumbled like a thunderstorm and cracked like lightning. It mesmerized me, pulled me, filled me somehow. I had to find this radio preacher, this John Easter Youthbone. He seemed well versed in apocalyptic matters, but I didn't need more data. I was going to burst if I soaked up more data! I had to see him face-to-face. As if compelled by instinct, I sought out his lair.

With a blare of trumpets that must have been taken from an old biblical-epic movie, he returned to the airwaves. "I'm back, ladies and gentlemen, brothers and sisters," he began. "Your voice of authority as the millennium approaches. This is John Easter Youthbone, End-Times Radio. Coming to you on WWEA—which can stand for either "World Without End, Amen" or "We Wait Eagerly for Apocalypse," take your pick. Ha *ha*, good evening. Why do I sound so happy? Because, friends, the end of the world is almost here, and that means salvation for those of us who heed the news. I plan on going to heaven, how 'bout you?"

I listened attentively for any clues of his whereabouts. I was in luck. Apparently his station was only a few miles away, on a county highway outside of Slagtown. I changed direction as quickly as I could.

"And now, here are the closing averages on today's index. I'm not talkin' about the Dow Jones Index, friends, because money will not buy you any sort of protection when the end comes. I'm talkin' about John Easter Youthbone's own End-Times Index, charting the conditions that must be in place for the apocalypse to come. Remember, rising averages mean a better chance for the end of it all."

TODAY, *PEACE IN ISRAEL* HELD STEADY, WHILE *PLAGUES* FELL ONE AND A HALF POINTS WITH REPORTS OF NEW TREATMENTS FOR THE AIDS VIRUS. *ONE-WORLD GOVERNMENT* IS UP A SOLID TWO POINTS WITH NEWS OF U.N. HUMANITARIAN MISSIONS TO CENTRAL AFRICA. *SPIRITUALISM AND THE OCCULT* ARE UP HALF A POINT, AS HALLOWEEN APPROACHES. AND A BIG GAIN FOR *HOMOSEXUALITY* TODAY, SURGING FOUR AND A HALF POINTS WITH THE RELEASE OF *THE BIRDCAGE* ON VIDEO. . . .

I sped single-mindedly toward the source of the signal. I passed through Slagtown but saw no signs of life. I began to feel a slight apprehension. Five miles outside of town, I spied a small cinder-block building with a lone car parked outside. Next to it was a radio tower with bloodshot lights blinking up to its zenith. This had to be the place. I parked and walked up to the plate-glass door. Stenciled on the front were the words "Youthbone Worldwide Enterprises, Inc. No Solicitors, Humanists, or Government Agents." I looked for a doorbell, but noticed that the door was jammed open by the throw rug inside. I pushed it open slowly and stepped in.

"You can, of course, subscribe to my *End-Times Index*," continued the preacher on the intercom in the building, "and it will cost you a lot less than those hustlers on Wall Street would charge you, with infinitely more valuable information. Just twenty dollars sent in to me will get you a subscription to the *End-Times Index* for a whole year. I'll even throw in a copy of my comprehensive 'Worldwide Conspiracy Chart' absolutely free. It's beautiful, friends, poster-sized and suitable for framing. They make great gifts, too."

Inside the lobby there was an astonishingly large portrait of the Reverend John Easter Youthbone, a large oil painting that looked exactly like a photograph. The man wore a three-piece suit with wide lapels and a watch chain, and looked out with a sunny smile and piercing eyes sunk low under his bushy single eyebrow. Any time you see a picture of a familiar radio voice, it's impossible to reconcile the picture you've built in your head with the one you see. This portrait exuded an authority that I recognized, however, and the overall impression was of a jovial sports coach who gets fired too often for various "improprieties." I needed to meet him in person, so I pushed onward, looking for the broadcast booth. Which wasn't hard, since this windowless bunker only had three rooms in it, not counting the bathroom.

Music began to play on the intercom, and within seconds I was surprised to see John Easter Youthbone burst out of the broadcast booth. No less surprised than he was to see me, though. He inhaled with a gasp when he saw me standing in the reception area, then put his hand to his chest. "Oh, man, you startled me," he said in a slightly accusing tone. "No one's ever around here after hours. Can I help you, son?"

If you have your own guess about the end of the world, don't parade around with a sandwich board. People will think you're a nut. Get a Web page instead. Then they'll think you're a high-tech researcher.

www.
buh-bye.
com

I looked at him, then back at his picture. Rather than a full head of multi-hued hair, I gazed upon a granitelike dome with white, wiry hair scattered over it. The uni-brow still flourished over his eyes, but the rugged, pink hue of his cheeks had been replaced by a pallid, slightly sweaty tint. The biggest shock of all was that the picture on the wall apparently was bigger than life-sized. John Easter Youthbone was only about four foot eleven.

"I'm not sure," I stammered. "I heard you on the radio while driving, and . . . and it seemed like you . . . had a lot of answers to my questions, I guess. I was getting so . . . worried out there. . . ."

"Well, you're welcome to hang around, friend. We don't turn away anybody here. Go wait in the broadcast booth, but don't touch nothin'. I got to see a man about a horse."

I found my way into the booth and sat down in a tall swivel chair. The room was dark except for a gooseneck lamp over Youthbone's place at the microphone and a clock on the wall, which read eight minutes to twelve. (Later I found out that the clock *always* read eight minutes to twelve. Youthbone used it as an inspiration, a memento mori, counting down to midnight, much like the clock on the cover of *The Bulletin of the Atomic Scientists*. He never cared what time it was; he just talked until he felt like going home, and was in again by six every morning.)

John Easter Youthbone came bursting into the studio and hoisted himself into his very tall chair. "No time to gab, commercial's done." In a snap he donned his headphones and slapped a button on his console. "We are back, here on WWEA, End-Times Radio. We are joined in the studio now by a young man I've just recently met, but feel like I've known all my life. Why'nt you introduce yourself to everyone listening out there, friend?"

He surprised me with this, I must admit. "Oh, really, no one out there wants to know," I stammered.

"I'm sure they would. We're all like family here."

"All right. It's James Finn Garner. That's my name."

"Well, good to have you with us tonight, Jimmy, even if your visit was a surprise. But it was no accident. We all know there are no such things as accidents, coincidences, or mere happenstance. There is only God's plan, which unfolds before us every second. Hey, do you know what time it is, Jimmy?"

"Um, the End Times?" Suddenly I felt like I was on *The Bozo Show,* with this call-response patter and this "Jimmy" stuff.

"Well, sure, that," laughed the preacher, "but it's also time for our Book Club of the Airwaves. Now, some of you out there have informed me that that woman on TV, Oprah Winfield, has taken to doing her own book club on her show, and that's fine, that's fine. If it helps people read, I suppose it's all right, as long as they're reading the truth about the future, and not a lot of secular humanist claptrap—pardon my French, Momma. The book we'll be discussing today is the new novel by Pat Robertson. The title is, fittingly, *The End of the Age,* and it's a wonderful story about the coming disasters. I laughed, I cried, I prayed. Have you read it, Jimmy?"

"No, Reverend Youthbone." Again with the childish answers.

He proceeded to give a rundown of the erstwhile candidate's recent potboiler.❡ Then he asked his listeners

❡ For the curious, here's a thumbnail of the plot: In the year 2000, a 300-billion-pound meteor crashes off the coast near Los Angeles, setting off tsunamis, volcanic eruptions, power outages, and riots. The hero, Carl Thorneberry, and his "normally ebullient" wife, Lori, have escaped to Colorado Springs, where they meet a ragtag bunch of believers in a place called El Refugio. (I had no idea

to call in and discuss the book. While we waited, he said, "So Jimmy, what did you think of the book?"

"Like I said, I didn't read it. Sounds like it would make a great Broadway musical, though."

Reverend Youthbone laughed surprisingly hard at my offhand comment. "Yes it would, yes it would, but we all know who runs Broadway, as well as the entire entertainment industry, don't we, folks? And they wouldn't want a story of this impact to make its way to a large audience." I tried to figure out who he was talking about. Who runs Broadway? The critics? The unions? Carol Channing? I hadn't come across those names in my research, but anything was possible by now.

The phones weren't ringing, so Youthbone began to talk about Pat Robertson's other novels, which sounded a lot like the latest one. His pale head shone like the moon under the gooseneck lamp. I passed the time doodling, drawing little football angels dumping bowls of plague and blood on Jimmy Johnson. Like a demented slide show, my mind still flashed with frightening images of the end. But for some reason I didn't find them upsetting now. They were like familiar parts of a landscape, and I felt like I was standing in the middle of that landscape. Suddenly, I was a player. I had a role in this, but what? Then, bit by bit, it started to dawn on me. . . .

"Because you know, friends, the Beast is among us today. Many people speculate on who the Antichrist

Robertson was bilingual, unless he's speaking in tongues, of course.)

Meanwhile in Washington, the rapid deaths of two presidents lead to the appointment of Senator Mark Beaulieu (who is really the Antichrist) to the Oval Office. The plucky band of born-again rebels somehow defeats Senator Antichrist's army (with the aid of some angels) and witnesses the descent from heaven of what looks like a flying saucer but turns out to be the New Jerusalem.

In the TV movie, I see Mark Hamill playing Thorneberry, with Richard Thomas as the Antichrist. Or the other way around. Works both ways.

might be, but before the Antichrist must come the Beast, he is what you call in Greek a harbinger. The Antichrist is sitting in the wings, but before he comes onstage, the Beast will have to make himself known. Jimmy, do you have any guesses about the identity of the Beast?"

I wished he'd quit asking me questions; his chipper manner and ghostly appearance were starting to unsettle me. "Many ideas are currently being kicked around, um, Reverend Youthbone, with varying degrees of plausibility."

"So, in light of those theories, what's your opinion?"

"I really . . . Each theory has . . . It's hard for me . . ." Visions flashed. Locusts. Dragons. Nancy Reagan. But somehow I felt in control.

John Easter Youthbone's sweaty head leaned forward and glowed under the lamp. "Spit it out, son. You know something, I can tell. What's your gut say? Who is the Beast?"

"Reverend Youthbone," I said, "it looks like the Beast is . . . me."

Did I really say that? The person who can't bring himself to yell at a hockey game, and I'm the Beast? Well, the signs. The obsession. The visions. It made sense. I had to say it. . . .

"That's an interesting idea, Jimmy. Let's explore it. You say you're the Beast of the Revelation, but you look like a pretty normal character to me. Where's your evidence? You are described as having the body of a leopard and the feet of a bear, for example. And frankly, I don't see it. Is this merely symbolic? Is there something more tangible?"

I unbuttoned my coat to show him my sweatshirt, which I'd bought at a high school rummage sale. The Reverend read it out loud: "The St. Leonard Leopards. Hmm, impressive. And your feet?"

A whole rack of these brochures was sitting in John Easter Youthbone's reception area. Looks pretty posh!

Tribulation Acres

The Ultimate Vacation Hideaway

Whoops! Missed the Rapture? Now what? You know you've been a good Christian, but maybe you don't want to spend the Tribulation playing "Army" with a bunch of yahoos in some damp hut in the mountains. You want to enjoy the time you've got left before you enter the pearly gates of the New Jerusalem. Now, at Tribulation Acres, you can be treated like the Chosen Elect you are!

One Upfront Fee!

Your money's no good at Tribulation Acres. Once you've paid for your reservation, everything is on the house. No tattoo bar codes, subcutaneous magnetic chips, or Marks of the Beast allowed.

A Safe Haven in Troubled Times!

Tribulation Acres is protected by a state-of-the-art security system and specially trained security force. The armies of the Antichrist will never bother you! (DNA sample required upon registration.)

Plus All the Amenities of a World-Class Resort!

• Independent fresh water supply! Don't worry about wormwood poisoning!

• Locust-free! Pestilence-protected!

• River Jordan–shaped pool!

• Full exercise facilities and 18-hole golf course!

• Amusement park for the kids, featuring the Four Horsemen Steeplechase, Tame the Dragon, and Ezekiel's Wheel!

RESERVE YOUR PLACE TODAY!
THE END TIMES HAVE NEVER BEEN SO GOOD!

© Youthbone Resorts International, Inc.

I looked down and lifted my foot into the light. "I've got my new boots on. They're Kodiak boots."

Reverend Youthbone took this in stride. "Kodiak boots. And as you good listeners know, a Kodiak is another name for the Alaskan brown bear. And I can attest that this man is also wearing orange and blue socks printed with the words 'Chicago Bears.' Another point in your column. But you can't just dress the part of the Beast. What other proof have you got? The Beast has ten horns, seven heads, seven crowns. Can you explain any of that? The crowns?"

"I've had a lot of dental work done recently."

"And the ten horns?"

"I have a pretty extensive collection of Miles Davis recordings."

"What about the seven heads?" asked Reverend Youthbone, with growing interest.

Multiple personality disorder? Extra bathrooms in the house? Hair weaves? "Did I mention that I collect antique ventriloquist dummies?"

The host shook his head and chuckled. "Man, you are one strange dude. For those of you just tuning in, this is John Easter Youthbone, End-Times Radio, live in the studio with James Finn Garner, and we are trying to determine whether he is a famous figure in the apocalypse. Now, Jimmy, the best minds in eschatological studies have determined that the Beast was probably born in the 1960s, somewhere in the Middle East. Does this apply to you?"

"The date is right," I explained, "but I was born in Detroit, which I guess is technically Middle West instead of Middle East. However, many people from the Middle East have relocated in the Detroit area, so it's just possible that in the maternity ward someone mistook the baby in the next bassinet for me." I paused. "It's a theory, anyway."

Youthbone looked me over more carefully, his beady eyes narrowing even further. "You're Irish, aren't you?"

"Yes, why?"

"While you've been here, I've been playing with the letters in your name, looking to see what they'd spell out in anagrams. It's a little game I play to amuse myself. I can't get anywhere with 'James,' but do you know the Irish version of that name?"

I had to think for a moment. "Seamus."

"Correct!" he said, startlingly loud. "And you can rearrange 'Seamus Finn Garner' in a number of interesting ways. For instance, 'N. Renames U Sir Fang.' Certainly a beastly sentence. If I may call you 'Sir Fang' for the moment, who might 'N.' be?"

"Nostradamus, of course! I hadn't . . ."

"Of course! And you seem to think of yourself as some sort of humorist, but your name really spells 'Amuser? Inner Fangs'!"

"You know," I said, getting into the swim of things, "it's also 'Grief's Annum Nears.'"

"And, as I remember those brave patriots defending themselves against the New World Order up in Montana, 'Sang Freeman's Ruin.'"

"And don't forget: 'Snaring Fur Enemas.'"

We both puzzled over that one. Finally, Youthbone said, "Well, the proof is piling up, nevertheless. Listeners, this is indeed a momentous night. Call us now with your questions. Jimmy, I must admit, you've almost convinced me, but something important is still missing. Tell me, what's your number?"

"I'd rather not give it out over the air, Reverend, especially after this little bit of news. I'd get phone calls at all hours——"

"Not your phone number, ya hellspawned fool! What about your mark, your 666?"

"My last name has six letters," I offered. "So does Seamus."

"But what about the 'Finn'?"

"Finn, Finn . . ." I searched for something. "'Fin' is a nickname for a five-dollar bill, so that gets us to 656. That's pretty close."

"656. No, that won't work. There must be another way. The numerical value of the letters in your name is 184—can't do much with that."

"Try the numbers on the phone keypad," I offered.

Youthbone scribbled a moment. "Comes out to 81, which is 18 backwards, and 18 is the sum total of three 6's."

"Wait a minute!" I slapped my forehead. "I am so dumb. I forgot to tell you: Finn isn't my real middle name. It's really Edward."

"Seamus *Edward* Garner?"

"Six . . . six . . . six."

Youthbone slammed his hand on the table. "I can't believe it! This is a red-letter day on End-Times Radio, friends! This man comes off the street into our studio, and it turns out that he's the Beast of the Revelation! This is too much!! Call your neighbors, everybody, and have them tune in! Tell me, how did you pick our program? You could have probably gotten on the *Today* show or something and reached many more listeners."

"Well, I can't say it was an accident, because there's no such—"

"Listeners, can you believe our luck? The Beast, right here in our studio. The end is coming, and it's coming to you first on WWEA! Do you have questions for the Beast? I know I do! Phone us right now with your questions, comments, or just to chew the fat. Who knows when you'll get this opportunity again? I've got a few things to start with—"

Before he could finish his sentence, the room went dark. Next we heard a large bang outside the studio. I didn't move in the pitch black, but an excited Youthbone kept talking. "Wow. What's that they say—'It never rains but it pours'? The bombs have already started dropping, haven't they?"

"It would make sense, I guess. I should apologize, this is all rather new to me."

"Aha, here it is," said Youthbone, and switched on a large camping flashlight. The light was almost shocking after the utter blackness. He shined it on me. "Well, Mr. Beast, shall we go outside and inspect your handiwork?"

He kept talking as we made our way outside to watch the world's imminent destruction. "If you'da asked me, I would've thought there'd be more time between your public announcement and the start of the tribulation. I mean, come on, five minutes is hardly enough for a person to prepare. So, it's finally here, huh? Looks like I didn't make the Rapture. Oh, well, time to wait out the Tribulation. Head for the hills. Good thing I checked the propane at my shelter over the weekend. Truck loaded and ready to go. Just pick up a few magazines from the lobby and some coffee filters, and I'll be all set."

The air was very still when we emerged from the building. The faint smell of something burning was in the air. No cars were on the road. No lights were visible except for the stars, which to all appearances had stayed in their place. "Kind of anticlimactic," Youthbone mumbled. "Or is this just a lull before things really start happening?"

"Beats me. Listen, this is all really strange. I didn't ask for this. I'd prefer to live a more private life. I don't know if I—" We heard another crash behind the building that made us both jump. "Should we go investigate?" I asked.

"Well," he laughed, "you're the Beast! Hee *hee*, I never thought I'd get to say that."

The gravel crunched beneath our feet as we rounded the corner. The beam from Youthbone's flashlight bobbed ahead of us along the ground. We saw things moving just ahead; then the light caught the tails of three raccoons running away from us. They were huge, big as dogs, and gave both of us a start.

Youthbone turned his beam to the left. The dumpster behind the building had been ransacked by the little bandits, with boxes and garbage thrown everywhere. A hot water heater lay on its side. "Aw, Sugar Jets. Where'd that water heater come from? Who's been using my station as a dump?"

Nocturnal nuisance or demonic destroyer?

The burnt odor was now much closer and quite nauseating. "Reverend Youthbone, what's that awful smell?"

He swung the light in a circle around us, then walked to the other side of the dumpster. In a few steps we stood next to a utility pole, looking down at our feet. There we saw what had caused the blackout: the charred remains of a raccoon, who had climbed the pole and touched off the power lines. It wasn't a pretty sight.

John Easter Youthbone gave a short bark and kicked viciously at a piece of garbage on the ground. This meant no bombs, no Tribulation, no end of the world for now. Which was not welcome news for the diminutive preacher.

"Some Beast you are!" he screeched at me. "Swindler! Fraud! If there's anything I hate more than a False Messiah, it's a False Beast!"

"I'm sorry, I'm sorry. I know you had your heart set on the apocalypse. So did I."

He barked some more and stomped his foot again and again. I felt pity for him, so heartbroken. He came up and shined the flashlight right in my eyes. "Who sent you here? Who sent you to make a fool of me? The United Nations? The Trilateral Commission? Jack Van Impe? Yeah, that's the kind of trick Van Impe would pull."

"No, no," I tried to console him. "I was out driving tonight, and I just happened to catch your show."

"But what about the evidence? How could we be wrong with so much evidence? Your background, your name. . ."

"Well, Reverend, have you ever done any anagrams for your name?"

"Of course I have," he snapped impatiently, "but the only significant arrangement is 'O shut, Trojan honeybee'!"

"'No, John, you're the Beast.'"

"Come again?"

"Look at your name," I said. "John Easter Youthbone: 'No, John, you're the Beast.'"

He slowly lowered the light from my eyes. I could see by his expression that he was double-checking and triple-checking my anagram. His anger visibly subsided, and was replaced by a faraway look. He repeated the words softly, then handed me his flashlight and began to walk toward the woods in the distance. I shined the beam on him and watched as his slow walk grew quicker, then became a jog, then a desperate, full-out sprint. In less than a minute, he was gone.

I bent down to examine what was left of the raccoon. The poor creature had probably been as unaware of his real fate as the Reverend John Easter Youthbone. A small fate, sure, in the overall scheme of things, but still important and still irretrievable. Maybe in the final analysis, your apocalypse is just a matter of perspective.

Or something like that.

Or not.

Acknowledgments

I want to thank the following people for their help and support during the writing of *Apocalypse Wow!* The world would never have ended without them.

Bill Rosen, for seemingly infinite faith and good humor, and for keeping the wolves at bay

Suzanne Gluck, for help in constructing an entire project out of two words

Pat Byrnes, for revealing my true nature

Adam Stewart, for finding answers to questions that hadn't been asked yet

Janice Easton, for reminding me why I had to work so hard

Marsinay Smith, for (generally) laughing at my jokes

The Secret Brotherhood Behind Everything, for sending the lovely cheese basket

Everyone who read chapters and assured me I wasn't losing my mind

And, most important, to **Lies**, for humor, understanding, patience, encouragement, and everything else. This book is for you.